Social Security and Medicine in the USSR
A Marxist Critique

Social Security and Medicine in the USSR

A Marxist Critique

Vicente Navarro
The Johns Hopkins University

Lexington Books
D.C. Heath and Company
Lexington, Massachusetts
Toronto

Library of Congress Cataloging in Publication Data

Navarro, Vicente.
    Social security and medicine in the USSR.

    Bibliography: p.
    Includes index.
    1. Medicine, State—Russia—History. 2. Social security—Russia—
History. 3. Communism and medicine. I. Title.
RA412.5.R9N38   362.1'0947   77-227
ISBN 0-669-01452-4

Published simultaneously in Canada

Printed in the United States of America

International Standard Book Number: 0-669-01452-4

Library of Congress Catalog Card Number: 77-227

To the Cuban Revolution, which has opened
a new era in the history of socialism.

Contents

x

List of Figures

List of Tables

Introduction

The Nature of this Volume

The 1917 October Revolution in Russia opened a new era in the history of humanity, starting a process that has affected all other societies since then. Because of its importance and significance, many analyses have been made of that and of subsequent events which determined the creation of the Soviet Union. Of these analyses, the most frequent ones in the Western world have been those which are based on the Weberian tradition, analyses that in the case of some authors have frequently deteriorated into a vulgar but rewarding anti-Sovietism which received much applause and support in the cold war's centers of power. With very few exceptions this situation has been particularly prevalent in the health sector, where most of the undeniable achievements made in the health and social security sectors of the Soviet Union were quickly dismissed as being largely the result of the fantasies and delusions considered typical of what was frequently defined as the world of Leniniana. Indeed, this unfortunate cold war spirit, much in evidence even today, was not the best intellectual environment for the analysis and study of what was presented as the "adversary." Accuracy and scholarship are not values appreciated in the art of soldiering. And a voluminous bibliography exists to prove it.

On the other side of the "intellectual barricades," there were those authors in the socialist tradition who perceived the Soviet Union as the "model" for the construction of socialism. Any adverse criticism of that model was perceived in that camp as helping its opponents. The *campagne de bataille* was thus clearly delineated, with no cracks allowed to show. And such an aversion to criticism appears also in the analysis of the health sector in the Soviet Union. Writers in the socialist tradition and style included the Webbs and the great Henry Sigerist, professor of history at Johns Hopkins. Actually, Sigerist's studies of the health sector in the Soviet Union constitute the most informative, detailed—and, some may convincingly say, uncritical—reporting of that experience in existence from this second group of authors.[1] Sigerist's work will be remembered for a long time. Let me add here that will it is easy *now* to be critical of those socialist authors for their unbalanced analyses of Soviet reality, still, one has to put oneself in the spirit of those years when the Soviet Union represented the only socialist state in the world struggling to survive; had played a decisive role in the victory over the Nazis; and was assisting other nascent socialist revolutions like that of the Chinese, which is much acclaimed today. Against this background, their silence toward any apparent weakness of the Soviet model is, although not excusable, understandable. Moreover, the personal sacrifice that this second group of authors—including Sigerist—experienced in terms of the McCarthyite repression in the United States puts them intellectually (and, I would add, morally) miles above the first group of Soviet analysts whose easy criticism was so generously rewarded. Courage and integrity are values to applaud. Opportunism is a value to abhor.

Today, new developments have taken place in the world that allow a better and more detailed appraisal of the historical meaning of the Soviet Union and of Soviet medicine by authors within the socialist tradition of writing. One development is the appearance on the horizon of history of other roads to socialism—China and Cuba—that, although influenced by the Soviet Union's experience and model of socialism, follow a different path today. Also, and enabling a closer scrutiny of the Soviet model, the initial dilution of the cold war has facilitated the thawing of past rigidities and a better look at Soviet realities. And that closer scrutiny shows that while the Soviet Union has achieved great successes in industrialization, urbanization, the raising of living standards, and achieving universal literacy, today, sixty years after the 1917 October Revolution, it remains as far away as ever from the aims of the founders, actors, and leaders of that revolution of creating "a true communal life, genuine equality, the abolition of class, rank, and distinction, the emancipation of women and sexual freedom, the liberation of arts, and the birth of a cooperative commonwealth in which men could at last find harmony among themselves and with their environment."[2] Indeed, as the well-known Italian Marxist author, Colletti, wrote recently, "the relationship between the idea of socialism and the reality of socialism [of the Soviet Union] is not much different from the relationship between the Sermon on the Mount and the Vatican."[3]

Why this gap between theory and practice? A central question, with no easy answers. The prevalent answer in our Weberian environment is the one given by conservative and liberal authors alike, i.e., the inevitable ossification of institutions in any society and the unchangeable nature of the human condition. Because of the frequency with which that interpretation is given, let me expand on it. The first thing we have to realize in understanding that interpretation is that it assumes an element of inevitability that transforms history into a deterministic and not a probabilistic and dialectical process. It presumes an almost fatalistic sense of history that reduces the role of human intervention to that of fitting into an ongoing and predetermined voyage. The motto for this group of authors could well be Lampedusa's saying that "the more things change, the more they remain the same." The popularity of this interpretation of the historical process among the well-established Weberian intellectual positions is due to its profound conservatism and defense of the status quo. Why indeed is there a need to change when everything in the end will remain the same?

Contrary to that interpretation, there is another one that sees history not as the culmination of predetermined forces but rather as a dialectical process in which historical forces—both material and ideal—interact and explain the nature and dimensions of historical change. According to this intepretation, the very same forces of liberation can become sources of oppression, depending on the material and objective conditions of the time. The analysis of history, then, is the analysis of the interaction between what is ideologically desired and what is materially possible. And in this view of reality, the current gap between the reality of the present-day Soviet Union and that of its founders is not the inevitable result of the unchanging and unchangeable human condition, but rather—as will be described in the following chapters—the result of the interaction between the unique material conditions of the Soviet Union in different time periods and the ideological positions of the leadership of the Communist Party during those periods. In the analysis of these forces, Marxist authors such as Bettelheim, Sweezy, Miliband, Colletti, Carlo, and others have contributed substantially to a better understanding of reality in the Soviet Union and also contributed to a further development of socialist theory. To them, I owe far more than simply a passing note of intellectual debt.

Still absent from this socialist reappraisal of the Soviet model, however, are analyses of the social security and health sectors. Here again, while finding in those sectors great achievements—to be shown in the following chapters—from the October Revolution to the present, both in the monumental increase in the overall number of resources and in the improvement of the distribution of those resources, still, as I will also illustrate in this volume, medicine in today's Soviet Union presents clear signs of alienation, undemocratic control, and inequitable distribution of resources, a bourgeois and individualistic interpretation, and hierarchicalization and discrimination in the health sector, all of which are phenomena and developments that typify the health sectors in capitalist societies and that clearly oppose and contradict the ideals of socialism.

The aim of this book is to present both the pros and cons of that experience, with a historical description and analysis of the past and present conditions of the social security and the health sectors. Included as part of that analysis is a presentation of my thesis of the evolution of events in those sectors and a discussion of possible socialist alternatives.

Method of Analysis

In the analysis of the social security and health sectors in the Soviet Union, I have followed two approaches that I believe are unfortunately absent in most studies of those social sectors.[a] Indeed, in trying to understand the composition and distribution of resources in the health sector, for example, or as I have indicated elsewhere, the nature of that sector itself,[4] one is hampered by the great scarcity of literature, both sociological and medical, that would explain the shape and form of the health sector and the nature and distribution of

---

[a] I am using the term "social sectors" to describe the supportive sectors of the economy, specifically focusing in this volume on social security and health services.

resources within it—the tree—by the same economic and political forces that shape the entire political and economic system of that society—the forest. Medical care research appears to reveal what C.W. Mills,[5] Birnbaum,[6] and others have found in other areas of social research—a predominance of experts on trees who do not analyze the forest.

This focus on the health sector without analysis of the socioeconomic system that determines it assumes an autonomy and near independence of the health sector that is both unempirical and unhistorical. Moreover, it leads to conclusions that are also empirically invalid and ineffective policy-wise. This is most clear in international health studies, where pieces of and individual experiences in the health sector are usually perceived as meriting "export" to other countries. A recent example of this is the present attention given to the Chinese barefoot doctors' experience. Much has been written concerning that interesting use of personnel in the People's Republic of China. Consequent to that interest, many national and international agencies, including the World Health Organization, are encouraging the export of that specific Chinese experience to other countries. Oblivious of China's socioeconomic determinants that may explain the success of the barefoot doctors, those exporters have tried to transform what is basically a political phenomenon into a mere managerial one. Not surprisingly, the export of the Chinese barefoot doctors' experience has failed to grow in those countries where the socioeconomic determinants were different ones.[7] Indeed, that experience assumes and presumes a series of economic and political parameters that determine its success. The purpose in citing this example and many others is not to question the value of international studies, but rather to stress the great importance of analyzing the nature of the health sector within a country's broader economic and political parameters which determine it.

Consequently, in the analysis of the social security and health sectors in the Soviet Union, I have started with an analysis of the economic, social, and political forces that determine the nature of the Soviet society and of the social sectors within that society. And as part of that analysis, a most important factor is the changes that have occurred in the nature and type of the productive sectors of the economy. Indeed, in the Soviet system, as in any other system, the health sector is primarily a supportive sector, aimed at responding to the needs of the various productive sectors of the Soviet economy. The former cannot be understood without understanding the latter. Thus the need for detailed explanation of the latter prior to explanation of the former. Therefore, my analysis of the changes in the different historical periods in (1) the social security schemes and the health sector, (2) the nature, composition, and distribution of the health labor force, and (3) the state mechanisms of regulation and control is preceded in each chapter by an analysis of the changes in the economic, social, and political forces that determined them at that time period.

The other methodological approach is one that also remains unfortunately absent in much of today's social research. Indeed, despite the truism that the present is built upon the past, few analyses are based on a historical approach in which the present is perceived as a dialectical result of the past. For example, many studies concerning the structure of the Soviet health sector limit themselves to the presentation of the current structure, defining it for the most part as being well structured and well integrated into a comprehensive whole. A more historical approach, as presented here, however, shows that the structure of the Soviet health sector is an aggregate of different components which appeared independently and without coordination in various time periods, in response to specific needs and changes in the mode of production (usually referred to as the needs of the economy) as perceived by the political leadership of that time. It is only when the description of the present structure of the health sector is preceded by a historical analysis of its varying components and the forces that determine it that one can understand the current values and meaning of present experiences. Chapters 1 through 5 present this historical analysis of the evolution of (1) the means and mode of production, (2) class and political structure, and (3) the ideology that sustains and replicates items (1) and (2), and shows how items (1), (2), and (3) determined the evolution of the social sectors analyzed.

In summary, in this method of analysis the historical process is perceived as the result of the dialectical relationship between the material conditions of the society—the economic infrastructure—and the ideology of the dominant groups and/or classes in that society. Specifically in the case of the Soviet Union, the evolution of society resulted from the interaction between the material basis of development of that society—which defines the realm of the possible—and the ideology of the nobility in pre-Soviet Russia and the leading groups of the Communist Party in the Soviet Union that guided and led to the implementation of that which they perceived as possible. In other words, in order to understand the reality of the Soviet Union we have to study (1) the evolution of the means and mode of production in that society and how that production was and is structured, (2) how people in that society were and are grouped and relate to each other, i.e., what classes and groups existed in that specific society in those specific time periods, and (3) the ideas of the groups in that society.

An analysis of Soviet reality following this sequence, and which considers all those forces as interacting with each other and among themselves but in which the status of the material forces of production is of primary importance in interacting with the other forces, is one that applies the method of historical materialism and the one I have adopted. Indeed, I found that method of analysis far more useful in understanding the Soviet Union's past and present than the more prevalent type of analysis used in our literature of historical studies of medical care which fall under the category of what can be defined as personalistic or idealistic interpretations of history. According to this last group of analysts, the history of the Soviet Union is primarily the result of what its leaders believed. But, as I will present in the following chapters, the different stages of Soviet development were determined not only by what the leaders of the Communist Party believed and wanted, but, most importantly, by the material conditions of the Soviet Union that sustained that ideology. As we will see, for example, Stalinism was the result not only of the ideas of Stalin and of the Communist Party, but also of the objective material conditions of the Soviet Union at that time. Stalinism was far more than the ideas of one individual. It is thus precisely to avoid this easy and misleading conclusion (shared by many among present Sovietologists) that one must study not only the ideology of the dominant groups of the Soviet Union but also the conditions that explain the perpetuation and legitimation of that ideology.

Following the above method of analysis, I present the evolution of social security, the health services, and the conceptualization of medicine in pre-Soviet Russia (Chapter 1), in the period of War Communism (Chapter 2), during the New Economic Policy (Chapter 3), in the period under Stalin (Chapter 4), and the time after Stalin (Chapter 5). That historical analysis leads to a better comprehension and understanding of the present structure of the Soviet health sector (Chapter 6) and the health labor force (Chapter 7), as well as of the rationale for Soviet state intervention in the health sector (Chapter 8) and the nature of that intervention (Chapter 9), i.e., the characteristics of the process of decision-making and planning, and of the regulatory machinery in that state intervention in the health sector.

Throughout this volume, I have tried to analyze the possible contemporary implications of the evolution of social security and the health sector in the USSR not only for other societies which are presently in a period of transition from capitalism to socialism (or, as Marx and Engels said, from prehistory to history) but also for the socialist movement in capitalist societies. A summary of what I consider to be the main points of relevance discussed in this volume is presented in Chapter 10, an epilogue and the final chapter.

A Final Note on Tone and Style

Having described the rationale for the writing of this volume, the method of analysis used, and its content, let me finish by including a final note on tone and style. Indeed, I suspect that a likely response among some readers of this volume may be to "box" the author into some category. Where does he stand? Actually, until recently, the monopolistic domain of Marxist theory by what Henry Lefèbvre once called the "dogmatic Marxist" determined an underdevelopment of both theory and practice in the evolution of socialism. And as a result of that situation, we have an *internal* Marxism (the one that responds to one's own specific practice) that is considerably underdeveloped, while the *external* Marxism (the one that is generated and imported from a practice somewhere else) is considerably overdeveloped. A result of that situation is that socialist forces are grouped and allied according to pro- or anti-foreign models (e.g., pro-Chinese, pro-Cuban, pro-Soviet, etc.), a situation that is most unfortunate since it replicates an ideological rigidity that paradoxically is most un-Marxist. As Marx himself continuously stressed, Marxism could never be perceived as a dogma. And as Gramsci has added, when Marxism is perceived as such, it is the first sign of its decay. Indeed, there can be no monopolization by a country, group, party, or whomever of the theoretical and practical development of Marxism. Of course, this does not imply that we cannot learn from other countries' experiences. Quite to the contrary. And in that respect, one aim of this volume is to single out those forces that appeared in the Soviet Union's experience which may replicate themselves—both in their liberating and oppressive dimensions—in other socialist experiences as well. Indeed, in any liberating force there is always, by definition, the possibility of the opposite. This is why I dedicate this work to the Cuban Revolution, a most important liberating force in today's world, which is in the very new and initial stages of creating a new society and a new human being. And it is in that enormous liberating potential that there is also the possibility of its opposite; and the strengthening and weakening of those opposites depend on the forces here defined. It is in this dialectical situation, as the Cuban people of course are aware, that the analysis of other socialist experiences is of paramount importance.

Regarding style, I have tried to avoid the baroque style of writing unfortunately so prevalent in academic circles on both sides of the ideological spectrum. Indeed, the same criticism that C. Wright Mills used to make of the sociologist could be addressed to many socialist theoreticians today, for it seems that the sophistry of language in their theories tends to hide the lack of understanding of their nonexistent practice. I very much hope that I will succeed in avoiding this pitfall.

Since beginning this project three years ago, I have had the great benefit of assistance from many individuals, institutions, and international agencies. Numerous colleagues have assisted me in the collection and analysis of the data presented here. To all of them—too many to be mentioned here—I want to express my great appreciation for their invaluable assistance. Thanks are especially due to Professor Ronald Frankenberg, Chairman of the Department of Sociology of Keele University, for his extensive and valuable comments on the initial manuscript, and to Dr. Felix Gutzwiller for preparing figures 8-2 and 8-3.

I also want to express my deepest thanks to Janet Archer, Pat Santora, and Christopher George for editing my initial English (with Catalan accent) manuscript and to Jane Seitz and Mimi Yacoub for translating my unintelligible handwriting into a readable form.

1

Pre-Soviet Russia

George Bernard Shaw used to say that wars bring some modernizing effects to belligerent countries. This seems to have been the case with Russia subsequent to her defeat in the Crimean War (1853–1856). When the Czarist regime of Alexander II became aware that the main reason for Russia's defeat was the backwardness of her economy, its response was to modernize Russia according to a policy of (1) state-directed industrialization based primarily on foreign capital; (2) emancipation of the serfs to enable their geographical and occupational mobility, with their transition from rural peasants to industrial workers; and (3) creation of the Zemstvo or local authority structure aimed at strengthening the process of central administration, taxation, and social control over the village communities. Those economics and political decisions created the framework against which (1) the type and nature of the pre-Soviet social insurance programs, and (2) the distribution and composition of the pre-Soviet health services must be understood. Due to the importance of those changes for our subsequent discussions of social security and health services in pre-Soviet Russia, let me expand on each of them.

The Industrialization of Pre-Soviet Russia

In 1861, the year of the emancipation of the serfs and the date considered by most historians to mark Russia's emergence as a modern state, the industrial capacity of that country was based on a traditional iron industry situated in the Urals, a craftsman textile industry located in Moscow, and a handicraft industry in the Caucasus and Volga regions. To stimulate foreign capital investment, the Czarist state guaranteed a fixed rate of return on capital to foreign corporations and passed legislation creating protective tariffs for new industries. Attracted by those policies, British, French, German, and Belgian capital heavily penetrated such existing industries as textiles and created new industries such as steel, coal, and oil, located primarily in the main urban centers.

The role of the Czarist state in this industrialization was (1) to stimulate foreign investment through attractive fiscal and monetary policies; (2) to create and direct the infrastructure of services to enable the operation and flourishing of industry, e.g., the creation of a massive railway system; and (3) to develop, direct, and own those sectors of industry, e.g., armaments, that were of paramount importance to the security of the state. As a result of those policies, industrial production grew dramatically, at an annual rate of 5.72 percent from 1861 to 1913.[1] And in some areas such as oil, Russia's overall production in 1901 was even larger than that of the United States' total output. In spite of this impressive growth, however, at the beginning of this century Russia remained a backward country compared with the industrial states of the West. For example, in 1913 her overall industrial production was only 7 percent and her per capita production only 4.8 percent of that of the United States.[2]

The consequences of industrialization in Russia were (1) the growth of the industrial working class, and (2) the concentration of workers in large-scale industries and a few urban centers. Indeed, due to the process of industrialization, the number of industrial workers involved in heavy industry and mining increased from 800,000 in 1861 to 2,500,000 in 1913, representing approximately 1.41 percent of the Russian population in the latter year. Yet, as a percentage of the population, the industrial working class was small, reflecting a lower level of industrialization than in other Western countries. (In the United States, for example, industrial workers made up 11.6 percent of the population in 1910.)[3] And as a result of the concentration of capital in that process of industrialization, the industrial labor force was employed primarily in large-scale industries, with the majority of workers (53.5 percent) in factories with over 500 employees, the equivalent figure for the United States being 33 percent.[4] Of the 2.5 million industrial workers in 1913, 918,000 were employed in textiles, 385,000 in the metal industry, and 215,000 in mining.[5] Also, for the most part, those industries and workers were concentrated in a few areas of Russia, primarily in Moscow, the Vladimir provinces, and Petrograd, all of which were to play a key role in the 1917 October Revolution. Actually, the concentration of the working class in key sectors of industry, and in the few vital urban centers of Russia, explains why, in spite of its limited size, that class played a decisive role in that revolution.

The Changes in Rural Russia

The process of industrialization was greatly facilitated by the movement of the population from rural to urban areas, resulting in the presence of a large pool or unorganized, nonunionized, and cheap labor in the main urban areas of Russia. In fact, the number of persons living in urban areas increased from 3 million (5.5 percent of the population) in 1850, to 20 million (14.6 percent) in 1914, representing a degree of urbanization unprecedented in Russian history.[6]

That substantial movement of people from rural to urban areas was partially due to the demand for labor caused by the creation and expansion of urban-based industry as well as trades and services, but was also largely facilitated by the very poor conditions in rural Russia and the backwardness of her agriculture. While the 1861 emancipation of serfs legally liberated the largest sector of Russian peasantry (although only in part),[a] it represented neither economic nor political liberation, as the peasantry remained highly dependent for its survival on the large landowners who owned and controlled the majority of Russian land. The peasantry was predominantly landless, owning only 15 percent of the land in 1900.[7]

The majority of the large land holdings was devoted to the production of agriculture for exporting. Actually, at the beginning of this century one-third of world wheat imports originated in Russia.[8] The system of tenure was similar to the type of land ownership now existing in most South American countries, i.e., a latifundia structure in which a small percentage of the population—the nobility in the case of Russia—owned large land holdings devoted to exports, and the majority of the population—the peasantry—worked for the large land holders and cultivated the minifundia, land holdings too small for commercial use and providing only enough food for survival. Within this scenario, the living and health conditions of the vast majority of peasants were very poor indeed, working, as Gorki wrote, from sunrise to sunset for some bread and much misery.[9]

For the most part, the peasantry lived in villages under the Zemstvo system of government established in 1864 as part of the modernization campaign of Alexander II. Although designed in theory to decentralize government from central to local government, in practice it was an administrative measure aimed at further strengthening the nobility's political, administrative, and social control over the nascent petite bourgeoisie and peasantry. The local government, or Zemstvo, was a district assembly elected by the inhabitants of the district, but not on the basis of one person-one vote. The nobility represented 72 percent of the deputies elected, with merchants, tradesmen, and the professions representing 10 percent and the peasantry another 10 percent.[10] The local government was responsible for public health and medical care services, education, and administering the local prisons, and was financed through tax contributions, with the peasantry carrying most of the burden. Actually, peasant-owned land was taxed at a higher rate than that owned by the nobility, and heavy taxes were imposed on the landless peasantry. This situation of naked exploitation created much social unrest among the peasantry who demanded more land and the discontinuation of heavy taxation. It was out of concern and fear over such unrest that in 1906 the Provisional Government of Stolypin, after the first October Revolution in 1905, created the first rural reform, the main objective of which was to divide the peasantry by strengthening and expanding the class of land-owning peasants or kulaks, who would act as a buffer zone between the nobility and the majority of landless peasantry.[11]

---

[a]Although the serfs could no longer be bought and sold, they still had to pay high taxes to the nobility-controlled local government whose permission they needed to migrate from the village.

The Social Class Structure of Pre-Soviet Russia

As a result of the changes outlined above, the social structure of pre-Soviet Russia at the beginning of the century was largely agricultural in production and feudal in social character, with incipient signs of capitalism. As a result of its relatively late start toward capitalist development, Russia had not experienced an industrial revolution to the extent of that in Western Europe and the United States. Moreover, whatever increase in heavy industrial output that occurred was primarily generated, stimulated, and controlled not by the bourgeoisie, as in the rest of Europe, but the nobility and its Czarist state, which controlled the means of production, i.e., land and capital. Thus, the two main classes prevalent in capitalist industrial development in Western countries at that time—the bourgeoisie and the working class—were small in Russia, at least by European standards.

In brief, the social class structure of Russia was still largely feudal with only the beginning features of capitalism. At the top was the *land-owning nobility*, representing approximately 1.4 percent of the population (2,193,000), who lived in the magnificent and opulent style so perceptively described in Tolstoy's *Anna Karenina*, and which included the hereditary owners of large estates, senior government officials, and senior officers of the different organs of the state. Their power came from their control over the means of production of the Russian economy—the majority (over 70 percent) of the land, and large sectors of the industrial capital (primarily heavy industry)—and of the organs of the state, the centralized civil service, the armed forces, and the church. The Czar was the highest authority, legitimized by the Russian Fundamental Laws (1892) which decreed that "the all-Russian Emperor is an autocrat and unlimited monarch—God himself commands his supreme power be obeyed out of conscience as well as fear."[12] Sharing power with the nobility was the *bourgeoisie* which had grown dependent upon the nobility due to the role of the latter in industrializing Russia. The bourgeoisie included the capitalist entrepreneureal class of owners and managers of large industrial enterprises, representing less than one-half of 1 percent of the population, as well as the petite bourgeoisie, or middle class, which included tradesmen, merchants, civil servants, and the professions, representing approximately 4 percent of the Russian population.[13] In the rural areas, the petite bourgeoisie was augmented by the middle peasantry who represented about 10 percent of the population.[14]

At the other end of the social spectrum was the *working class*, including (1) industrial blue-collar workers (approximately 1.4 percent of the population); (2) service workers, including workers in transport and social services; and (3) workers in handicraft industries. Approximately 16.7 percent of the population together with their dependents, they represented the majority of wage and salary earners in industry, trades, and services.[15] At the bottom of the social spectrum was the *landless peasantry*, who worked for the nobility and the kulaks (land-owning farmers), who lived under conditions, superbly described by Tolstoy, Gorki, and many others, of continuously enduring misery. They represented over 70 percent of the Russian population.

The Political Determinants of the Social Security Program

Until 1905 the nobility had unchallenged control over all of the organs of the state apparatus and the Czar reigned with absolute power. The series of peasants' uprisings, workers' revolts, and even rebellions in the armed forces (as memorialized in Eisenstein's *Potemkin*) that took place in the very early years of this century in Russia culminated in the Moscow and Petrograd workers' uprisings of October of 1905, identified by Lenin as the rehearsal for the Soviet's October Revolution of 1917. The response of the state-controlled nobility to those uprisings was (1) a strengthening of the repressive policies through a brutal massacre of the working class, known as the Bloody Sunday Massacre, in which thousands of workers were killed; (2) the Czar's promise of civil freedoms with legalization of political parties, forbidden until then; (3) the creation of a consultative body, or Duma, with two houses, one appointed by the Czar and the other elected by electoral colleges based on social class, with the peasantry allowed to elect 43.4 percent, landlords 31.8 percent, townsmen (i.e., primarily tradesmen, state employees, and professionals) 22.4 percent, and the workers 2.4 percent of the membership (in that parliamentary scheme, the Duma had advisory but no legislative or executive power);[16] (4) the creation of social legislation to provide some measure of security in unemployment, disability, and sickness to certain sectors of the working class; and (5) the creation of the Rural Bank, entitled to favor credit to peasants for buying land. This latter policy was one component of the rural reforms aimed, as mentioned earlier, at creating a new land-owning sector within the peasantry, namely the kulaks. The Czarist government hoped that the kulaks would support the Czar and act as a buffer against the landless sector of the peasantry. Thus, in the Zemstvo government, the kulaks were granted a sharing of power with the nobility, establishing an alliance with the nobility against the landless peasantry.

Those state measures responding to the workers' and peasants' uprisings were consistent with the historical experiences in other countries as well; i.e., a combination of repressive and cooptive policies aimed at diffusing such threats. As the 1917 October Revolution showed, however, those 1905 responses were too little and too late to save the Czarist regime.

Representing the forces against the Czarist order was the bourgeoisie, whose political expression was the Constitutional Democratic Party (Cadets), and the Russian Liberal Party. The bourgeoisie favored the liberalization of the Czarist regime and the adoption of a parliamentary democracy based on the Duma. Its political program included the expropriation of land with indemnification to the landlords, the creation of protective labor legislation for child and female labor, and the setting up of a labor relations board to resolve industrial conflicts. Due to the already mentioned dependency of the bourgeoisie, this party was weak and not very large. To the left of this party were the three socialist parties that played a major role in the events that led to the 1917 October Revolution: the Social Revolutionary Party, the largest party subsequent to the legalization of all parties in 1905, which was an agrarian-populist movement demanding a cooperative socialist agricultural economy; and the two working-class-based or social democratic parties, the Mensheviks and the Bolsheviks. These parties, successors of the original Social Democratic Party, although sharing many of the same objectives, differed in strategy. The Mensheviks felt that Russia was not ready for socialism and that the feudal order should be transcended by the bourgeois order and then, and only then, by the socialist order. The rationale for this argument was that there could not be an immediate change from feudalism to socialism; rather the economy of Russia should go through the intermediate stage of capitalism. Thus, politically, the Mensheviks supported the Constitutional Democratic Party—the voice of the bourgeoisie—in its intent to establish the capitalist economy and the political bourgeois order, characterized by parliamentarianism as the prevalent political form. Its role was perceived as that of protecting workers' rights during the bourgeois revolution.

Led by Lenin, the Bolsheviks, while agreeing that feudalism could not be transcended by socialism and that a bourgeois revolution—establishing bourgeois democracy—was necessary, felt that that revolution should be led by the working class, not by the bourgeoisie itself. Consequently, the Bolshevik Party supported neither the bourgeois party nor the Czarist government, but fought them continuously.[17]

Social Security as a Campagne de Bataille in Pre-Soviet Russia

One of the areas of disagreement between Lenin's Bolsheviks and all other parties, including the Mensheviks, was on the nature and extension of social insurance programs and the political strategy for their implementation. Indeed, prior to 1917, the only social insurance schemes that existed were (1) the Social Acts of 1866 and 1892, requiring employers in mines and metallurgic establishments with large employment (representing the majority of such establishments) to provide free medical care to their workers;[18] and (2) the Industrial Accidents Act of 1903, requiring employers to provide disability cash benefits for workers in mines and large metallurgic establishments, excluding those working in small ones. Both acts were prompted by the aforementioned priorities given to industrialization and by the continuous industrial unrest and strikes among workers in the most militant sectors of the industrial working class—i.e., workers in the primary sectors of the economy, such as manufacturing—the majority of whom were working in large enterprises and in the main urban centers of Russia. Yet, as perceived by the working-class-based parties, the programs established by those two acts were limited in terms of benefits, small in terms of population coverage (dependents were excluded), and were administered by employers who frequently used their control over those programs to selectively coopt and divide the working force in their establishments. Because of their very limited nature and scope, those programs did not meet their primary purpose of coopting and integrating the industrial working class into the Czarist system. Rather, they further stimulated a discontent that culminated in the 1905 October Revolution that, although repressed, served to function as a warning to the Czarist regime. It triggered, among other responses, the debate that culminated in the Health and Accident Act of June 23, 1912, which instructed employers to provide and pay for cash benefits in case of work-connected accidents, general illness and death,[b] and allowed for employee participation in the administration of the general illness and death insurance programs to which they contributed.

Still, the limited benefits and narrow coverage—extending to less than one-fourth of the labor force[19]—of the 1912 scheme made it rather unpopular among large sectors of the working class, particularly considering the high degree of politicization that the class had achieved as a result of a long history of struggle, and their response and receptivity to a more attractive alternative, i.e., Lenin's social security schemes.

The working class, however, was not uniform in its response. The Mensheviks, whose main constituency was among the highly skilled and organized workers, e.g., printers, railwaymen, and steel workers in the modern industrial centers of the south, were dissatisfied with the 1912 act, but advocated an expansion of benefits rather than a qualitative change in the overall nature and control of social insurance. In these and other programs, the Mensheviks were evolutionist, preferring to follow the lead of the bourgeois parties, and to encourage the creation of capitalism. Thus, "the socialist revolution could be the work only of a strong proletariat; the Russian proletariat could become strong only through the development of Russian capitalism; Russian capitalism could be developed only through the victory of the bourgeois revolution."[20] In this process, then, the Menshevik Party was a conscious supporter of the bourgeoisie, favoring an evolutionary strategy and a gradual development of the social insurance programs.

Contrary to the Mensheviks, Lenin, the leader of the Bolsheviks, felt that the working-class-based parties should provide the active leadership in the process of revolutionizing the economic and social structures of Russia. Thus, in the 1912 Prague meeting of the Party set up to prepare for the Duma elections, the Bolsheviks (whose main constituency was the unskilled laborers of the mass industries, i.e., the heavy industry of the Petersburg region and the textile factories of Petrograd and Moscow) demanded a radical program whose implementation would have antagonized not only the nobility but the bourgeoisie as well. That program encompassed (1) political demands for equal and universal suffrage, freedom of speech and assembly, and separation of

---

[b]Benefits for work-connected accidents were exclusively paid by the employers, whereas benefits for general illness and death were jointly financed by employer and employee contributions.

church and state; (2) economic demands, including the eight-hour work day and land reform; and (3) *social demands*, calling not only for the most ambitious social reforms, but also for reforms that would have met with great resistance from the bourgeoisie. One of them was the demand for a radical change in the control of the insurance programs and a radical expansion in the benefits of the programs as proposed in the Social Insurance Act. Calling the 1912 act "an unworthy bill with a beggarly rate of compensation," Lenin demanded that a new bill be passed by the Duma which would contain the following principles:

1. It should provide assistance in *all* cases of incapacity, including old age, accidents, illness, death of the breadwinner, as well as maternity and birth benefits.
2. It should cover *all* wage earners and their families.
3. The benefits should equal full earnings and *all* costs should be borne by employers and the State.
4. There should be uniform insurance organizations (rather than organization by risk) of a territorial type and under the full management of the insured workers.[21]

Moreover, Lenin indicated that in the event that the 1912 act were implemented, the militants of the Bolshevik Party should agitate against the bill and use the organs of the program for their political purposes:

Should the Duma Bill become law in spite of the protest of the class-conscious proletariat, the Conference summons the comrades to make use of the new organizational forms which it provides (workers' sick benefit societies) to carry on energetic propaganda for Social-Democratic ideas in these organizational units and thus turn the new law, devised as a means of putting new chains and a new yoke upon the proletariat, into a means of developing its class-consciousness, strengthening its organization and intensifying its struggle for full political liberty and for socialism.[22]

It was the intention of Lenin to use the battle over expansion and control of the social insurance programs as a means for politicizing the working class. Social security, then, became a *campagne de bataille*, not resolved, at least in theory, until the second and successful October Revolution of 1917.

A passing but relevant point to make here is that Lenin clearly envisioned the possibility of using reformist campaigns as a way of politicizing the population. He pushed and fought for specific social legislation, demanding what would be defined in contemporary terms as "Utopian solutions." And he did it to show, first, the level to which the working class should aspire, and also to use that struggle for the "Utopian" as the means for politicizing that class. The wisdom of this Leninist strategy, clearly replicated today in the writings of André Gorz,[23] should not be lost to present socialist strategists.

Zemstvo Medicine, or the World's First Attempt to
Regionalize Medicine

In the annals of the history of medicine, Zemstvo medicine is presented as the first case in the world of organizing medicine and hospital care services on a large scale.[24] It is usually presented as a progressive and liberal attempt at providing care to large masses of the peasantry and as part of the modernization campaign started by Alexander II with the emancipation of the serfs in 1861.

Zemstvo medicine started with the reorganization of local government in 1864, as I described previously. In this reorganization, the country was to be divided into districts or *uchastocks*. Following these political divisions, Zemstvo medicine was supposed to provide basic primary care in dispensaries located in the districts, with more specialized care to be provided in the provincial hospitals. In that respect it was the first historical instance of regionalization of medical care. The dispensaries, or uchastock medical centers, were meant to be staffed by district physicians, assisted by feldshers. The former were physicians paid on a salary basis (from 1,000 to 1,500 rubles per annum) and employed by the district or Zemstvo government. The latter were a form of assistant-barbers who learned their craft practically by working with physicians.[25] It was only later, after the 1905 reforms, that they were given a two-year course of training in special military and medical schools. These district centers frequently had fifteen to twenty beds, mostly occupied by patients with infectious diseases, and were supposed to provide curative and preventive medicine to the limited degree that such measures were known at that time.

The provincial centers were usually provincial hospitals, with 60 to 300 beds, staffed, for the most part, by full-time, salaried doctors, assisted by feldshers. The overall desired staffing ratios, rarely achieved, were one physician to every 50 beds, and one feldsher to every 25 beds. In theory, the Zemstvo reform was intended to regionalize the provision of medical and hospital care, and to optimize and facilitate the provision of care to the population. That reform was an integral part of the regionalization of social services generally, including education, welfare, and health services.

The Socioeconomic Etiology of Zemstvo Medicine

In the not very extensive bibliography on Zemstvo medicine, three reasons are usually given to explain the motivation for that reform: (1) the need for increased productivity of the labor force through an improvement in the health of the productive sector of the population, i.e., health services as capital investment;[26] (2) the enlightenment of Zemstvo physicians, representing 15 percent of Russian physicians who were assumed to be socially motivated and populist in political behavior;[27] and (3) the general desire of the Czarist regime to continue and extend the overall modernization campaign started by Alexander II. It is highly unlikely, however, that Zemstvo reforms were implemented for the first two reasons. Indeed, they were primarily aimed at the rural population where the rate of unemployment was very large, whereas the most productive sectors were in the nascent urban areas among the industrial working class, whose gains in benefits and coverage of medical and hospital care were obtained, for the most part, independently of the Zemstvo reforms.

I would postulate, therefore, that far more important than the reasons enumerated above were (1) the Czarist nobility's increased concern that it was floating in a sea of disease, the diseased rural population; (2) its perception that its own health, or lack of it, was dependent on the overall health of the population (due to the introduction of the theory of infectious diseases in Russia at that time); and (3) the nobility's belief that "scientific medicine"—the latest modernizing influence coming from Europe—could, by reducing the number of epidemics affecting the overall population, reduce as well the risk of its own contamination. Supporting my interpretation, all accumulated evidence shows that the health conditions of rural Russia—where not only most of the Russian population, the peasantry, but also the nobility lived—were dismal. At the beginning of the Zemstvo reform, the rate of infant mortality was estimated (most likely conservatively) to be 500 deaths per 1,000 live births, with over one-fourth of the peasantry being inflicted with debilitating infectious conditions. Even as late in the Zemstvo period as 1914, about one-quarter of the population was suffering from typhus, typhoid fever, and smallpox.[28] Also, it was just prior to the starting period of Zemstvo reforms that the ideology of scientific medicine, which originated in Belgium, Holland, and Germany, became predominant throughout the European continent.[c] Scientific medicine was, then, a component of the new modernizing ideas that the Russian Czarist regime absorbed and incorporated for its own use. And an important part of scientific medicine was a belief in (a) the theory of infection and contamination of disease, and (b) the effectiveness of hygiene and medicine in controlling disease. Instructed by that belief, the nobility came to realize that it could not be insulated from the sea of epidemics and that its fate was tied to that of everyone. Thus the commitment of the Czarist nobility to provide care not only for itself but the entire population as well. But in this commitment, the medical services were supposed to be directed and controlled by the nobility through the Zemstvo government that the nobility controlled, and paid for and funded by the peasantry who financially supported that government. Indeed, the medical services were directed by the district and provincial governments that, as shown before, were controlled by the nobility. Only in the latter part of the

---

[c]The best known medical school in Europe, and the one most influencing the birth of Soviet medicine, was the school in Leyden, Holland, famous for its anatomic laboratory and visited by Peter the Great, himself an amateur surgeon.

nineteenth century did the Zemstvo government appoint a medical advisory council. Still, the executive power resided in the nobility-controlled local authorities. And while the nobility controlled the activities of that government (education, welfare, health, and prisons), these were paid for and funded through the heavy taxes imposed on the peasantry. Reflecting that pattern of control, the Zemstvo services were structured to benefit primarily the nobility, and only secondarily, very secondarily, the peasantry. For example, in the allocation of human health resources available to the population, the physicians were reserved primarily to serve the nobility, while the feldshers were to serve the peasantry. Needless to say, the former were perceived by the nobility to be the better qualified. As Mistskevich wrote, the nobility felt that "the peasant is not accustomed and does not need scientific medical assistance; his diseases are 'simple' and for this a feldsher is enough—a physician treats the masters, and a peasant is treated by a feldsher."[29]

In summary, then, the "best," as perceived by the nobility, was meant to take care of that class, and the feldsher to take care of the majority—the peasantry. Yet the peasantry, via taxes, paid for both of them. Moreover, the control of the delivery of medical care services by the nobility-controlled Zemstvo government was used by that class to optimize its control over the peasantry. The ills and diseases of the majority of the population were supposed to be cured and cared for by a medical care system controlled and administered by the nobility and based on scientific medicine.

Medicine and the Health Labor Force in Pre-Soviet Russia

The introduction of scientific medicine in Russia was one of the first of Western Europe's modernizing influences over Peter the Great's Russia.[30] With him, Russia entered the European scene both politically and culturally, and he himself visited most of the leading European medical teaching institutions at that time, and is reputed to have performed anatomy dissections. His regime also started the first medical school in Moscow in 1706, heavily influenced by the Leyden medical school. The main emphasis was on anatomy and on what McKeown has defined as the mechanistic approach to medicine, in which medicine is perceived as intervention aimed at repairing the pieces of the body to achieve a balance among its fluids and solids.[31] Thus, "nature was conceived in mechanistic terms, which led in biology to the idea that a living organism could be regarded as a machine which might be taken apart and reassembled if its structure and function were fully understood."[32] This mechanistic orientation in medicine had been the intellectual construct on which the ideology of scientific medicine was based. And that approach spread throughout Europe (and later on, with the Flexner Report, to the United States) as part of the scientific and industrial revolution in medicine. That mechanistic approach to medicine was very much facilitated, incidentally, by the prevalent ideology emerging from the industrial revolution that had, as its symbolic axis, the steam engine.

In Russian medicine, we find a situation similar to that found in the overall evolution of the means of production of the Russian economy. To the same degree that the industrial revolution was a latecomer to Russia, and then stimulated primarily by the nobility, mechanistic or scientific medicine (the equivalent to the industrial revolution in medicine) was also introduced relatively late, and upon its introduction was guided, directed, and controlled primarily by the Russian nobility, with the medical profession predominantly at its service. Also in medicine, reflecting the strong commitment by Alexander II to the modernization of Russia (the second wave of modernization after that following the Crimean defeat of the Russian army), and paralleling the very rapid growth of industrial production, there was a similar growth in the production of physicians in pre-Soviet Russia during the period 1861–1917. Indeed, to be patriotic was to be modern and to be modern was to follow the European mode of production of resources, both outside and within the health sector. Accordingly, the number of scientifically-trained physicians more than doubled from 1864 to 1913, increasing from 10,000 to 23,000 in that period.[33] Most of those physicians were located in the main urban centers, although with the Zemstvo reforms there was a substantial increase in numbers of physicians working in provincial towns and districts; the number of doctors working in rural districts increased from 756 in 1870 to 1,805 in 1890.[34] It is worth noting that, with the exception of those physicians who had received state assistance during their training, there was not a compulsory service for physicians to work with the Zemstvo authorities.[35] Instead, those authorities relied very heavily on incentives, such as (1) providing living quarters and free travel expenses; (2) raising the physicians' salaries of approximately 1,000 to 1,500 rubles a year by 25 percent every three to five years; (3) establishing pension funds for physicians' retirement, and (4), and very likely having the least effect, calling on the physician's patriotism and social motivation to serve the nobility and/or peasantry living in rural Russia. Indeed, the very poor living and practicing conditions of rural Russia, well described by Chekhov—a Zemstvo physician himself—had the effect of diminishing very rapidly any patriotism or social motivation that individuals who belonged to the petite bourgeoisie of pre-Soviet Russia may have felt initially. Those incentive strategies seem to have had little effect on redistributing resources in pre-Soviet Russia. In 1917, 92 percent of all physicians were practicing in the large cities where less than 17 percent of the Russian population lived.[36]

Complementing the increased production of physicians in the period 1861–1917, there was a substantial growth in the number of midwives and feldshers. The former were trained in medical schools of Moscow and Petrograd established as early as the mid-1700s, and were serving primarily the nobility and petite bourgeoisie. The latter had ad hoc practical training, and it was not until the beginning of this century that formal training, attached to military schools, was developed. They served primarily the peasantry and their greatest growth took place during the Zemstvo reforms and in the rural areas. Including midwives, their numbers grew from 2,794 in 1870 to 6,778 in 1890.[37]

The Ideological and Social Functions of Scientific Medicine in Pre-Soviet Russia

Much that has been written on the origins of scientific medicine in Europe has been by authors who consciously or unconsciously belonged to the Hegelian or idealistic school, i.e., authors who interpret the origins of scientific medicine as a result of the ideas and ideology prevalent at the time and period of birth of that type of medicine. Let me add, parenthetically, that this Hegelian interpretation is also the most prevalent interpretation of social change among our social historians and analysts. They assume that ideology and its manifestations are the main forces of history.

But as Marx and the historical materialists have indicated, those idealist interpretations beg the question of how a certain ideology becomes the prevalent one in a society. In other words, they avoid the analysis of (1) the actual material reasons behind the flourishing of an ideology, i.e., the economic infrastructure and the power relations that that infrastructure determines, and (2) the social function of that ideology. Indeed, as Colletti has indicated,[38] Hegelians do not deal with and do not touch on the issue of who controls and benefits from the creation, perpetuation, and legitimation of a specific ideology. Historical materialists do. And in Marx's interpretation, the prevalent ideology of a society is the one that is convenient and benefits the existing power relations of that society, and thus of the dominant class:

The ideas of the ruling class are in every *epoch* the ruling ideas: i.e., the class which is the ruling *material* force of society is at the same time its ruling *intellectual* force. The class which has the means of material production at its disposal, has control at the same time over the means of *mental* production.[39]

Indeed, to understand the ideological edifice of a society (and medicine is part of it), we have to understand the pattern and nature of control of the means of production in the society that the ideological construct is aimed at sustaining. Let me hasten to add here that that relationship between the material forces and ideology is not a linear and deterministic one, but rather a dialectical one in which ideology also interacts with the material infrastructure that is sustained by that ideology. To quote Engels:

Political, religious, juridical, philosophical, literary, artistic, [and I would add medical], etc., development is based on economic development. But all these react upon one another and also upon the economic bases. It is not that the economic situation is *cause, solely active*, while everything else is only passive effect. There is, rather, interaction on the basis of economic necessity, which *ultimately* always asserts itself.[40]

In this dialectical relationship, the material forces and *not* the ideology are the main motor of social change, the ones that ultimately assert themselves. But neither are the other forces passive.

In this historical analysis, scientific medicine is no exception. Indeed, scientific medicine served a social and ideological function that was convenient to the dominant class, i.e., the nobility in Russia and the industrial bourgeoisie in Western Europe. The nobility controlled, via the state, both the content—the ideology of scientific medicine—and the instruments of medicine—the medical care system. According to the ideology of scientific medicine, disease was supposed to be a biological and individual problem, not a social and political one, i.e., disease was perceived as a dysfunction of the body that had to be controlled or eliminated by therapeutic intervention aimed at the individual. Thus, the cure for disease was perceived primarily as changes taking place in the patient, not changes occurring in the social and political systems. Actually, had the peasantry and the majority of the Russian people seen it otherwise, that is to say, had they realized that the solution to the problem of the existing sea of disease required changes in the social and political systems, this perception would have represented a clear threat to the nobility. Thus, the individualistic vision of scientific medicine had an ideological function that explains its rapid adoption by the Czarist nobility. It transformed a political problem into a more individual one that could be solved by medical care intervention which was controlled by the nobility, i.e., the ills and disease suffered by the majority of the Russian population were supposed to be cured and cared for by a medical care system that was regulated and administered by the state and controlled by the Russian nobility. Thus the medical care system contributed to the legitimation of the power relations in Czarist Russia.

Let me further clarify that this dialectical materialist interpretation of the absorption and diffusion of scientific medicine by the Russian nobility does not imply nor subsume any conspiratorial theory of history. In other words, it does not assume that the nobility deliberately subscribed to and diffused the ideology of scientific medicine to keep its power. Rather, due to the control of the subject and content of medicine by the Russian nobility, that control determined that the content of medicine—scientific medicine—and the type of delivery—medical care system—had to be one that would primarily benefit the dominant class and the power relations of pre-soviet Russia.

2

The Soviet Revolution and War Communism: 1917-1921

The October Revolution and After

Few events in the twentieth century have had more historic relevance and greater impact than the series of events that took place between February and October of 1917 in Russia—a series of events referred to as the Soviet Revolution.

The February Revolution overthrowing the Romanov dynasty was a spontaneous outbreak of both workers and large sectors of the peasantry exasperated by the privations of war against Germany (World War I) and the unequal distribution of its burdens.[1] Leadership in that uprising was assumed by the workers of Petrograd, the most politicized among the workers, and was constituted by the Petrograd Soviet of Workers' Deputies, a council elected by factory workers which included Mensheviks, Social Revolutionaries, and Bolsheviks.[a] This council was a revival of the Petrograd Soviet that had played a brief role in the uprising of 1905. It was not the Soviets' intention, however, to take over state power. In fact, those Soviets were later dominated by the Mensheviks whose immediate political program was not one of socialist but of bourgeois revolution, based on their belief that Russia was ready for the latter but not the former. Thus they surrendered their power to the Provisional Government, dominated by the bourgeois parties, primarily the Cadets, that had been established in Moscow. The primary objective of that government was to win the war against Germany, fighting on the side of the Allies and postponing all socioeconomic and political reforms until victory.

The arrival in European Russia of the exiled Bolshevik leadership—Lenin from Switzerland, Trotsky from New York, and Stalin from Siberia—had a great impact during the following months. It strengthened the Bolshevik Party and its appeal to the workers increasingly dissatisfied with the Provisional Government. The Bolsheviks demanded immediate peace with Germany and the transfer of power from the Provisional Government, led by Kerensky, to the Soviets or councils of elected representatives of workers, peasants, and soldiers, which had remained as parallel institutions to those of the state. Their slogan, "All power to the Soviets," had great appeal to the workers. Among their immediate demands were the establishment of democratic reforms, an

---

[a]These party members served on such councils as individuals, not as party representatives. Actually, the revolutionary partys' leaderships were caught quite by surprise by the evolution of events.

15

eight-hour work day, and implementation of social security programs as enunciated in the Prague Party Program of 1912.

The following events escalated very rapidly. The Provisional Government, composed at that time of Cadets, Mensheviks, and Right Social Revolutionaries,[b] banned the Bolshevik Party, destroyed its presses, and imprisoned its leaders. In response, the Bolshevik Party called for an armed insurrection against the Provisional Government. Moreover, it encouraged and supported the spontaneous takeover of the factories by the workers and of the land by the landless peasants. And on the twenty-first of October of that year, the Bolsheviks seized the Winter Palace, forcing Kerensky to flee. It is symptomatic of its priorities that the first decrees signed by the new government—dominated by the Bolsheviks and the Left Social Revolutionaries—were the peace offer to Germany (not accepted until 1918), the legalization of the peasantry's and workers' takeovers, and *the establishment of a comprehensive social security system.*

With these events the first and most difficult years of that revolution began, typified by profound changes in the productive and social sectors of society. Among the former were (1) an increase in the takeover of factories by the industrial workers following a spontaneous movement in which, at the end of the period, all factories having more than five employees were taken over either by industrial workers' committees or by the state; (2) nationalization of the key industries of the economy—coal, iron, oil, steel, chemicals, and textiles—by the new government; and (3) the distribution of land among peasants, first through the establishment of peasants' cooperatives and, in 1920, by creating state collective farms.[2] Among the changes in the social sectors were (1) the goal of implementing comprehensive social insurance administered by the insured, and (2) restructuring of the medical sector, with local control of the health sector by the Soviets.

All those changes took place amidst great obstacles presented by a civil war referred to as War Communism in which the Red Army, directed by Trotsky and controlling only one-seventieth of Russian territory, fought the White Army, representing a coalition of forces of the old nobility and the Provisional Government supported by Allied forces; an economic blockade imposed against the Bolshevik government by most European countries; and peasant resistance to the creation of state collective farms, or kolkhozs, with sabotage in the production and distribution of food.[c]

As a result of these events, the previously-mentioned economic and social policies met with innumerable problems and difficulties, not the least of which

---

[b]The Social Revolutionaries had split into two groups: a left wing, which sided with the Bolsheviks, and a right wing, which sided with the Mensheviks.

[c]According to Carr, a conflict arose in the land reform between the Left Social Revolutionaries, who favored private ownership of land by the peasants after the initial reform, and the Bolsheviks, who favored the creation of state collectives.

was the massive abandonment of the cities by large segments of the population migrating to rural areas in search of food. The urban population declined from 25 million to 20 million, with an overall decline in the Russian population of 9 million.[3]

From Social Insurance to Social Security

The advent of the Bolsheviks to power meant the intent to implement the 1912 Prague Program for social security enunciated in the party program at that time. Lenin personally took leadership in its implementation, since he had been instrumental in its drafting and felt that after employment and job security, the Russian people most wanted insurance against unemployment, accident, disease, and old age. As the Bolshevik program indicated, "The Russian proletariat has placed on its banners 'Full Social Insurance for Wage Workers' as well as for the city and village poor."[4] Four days after taking power, the Bolshevik-dominated government issued a communiqué announcing a new social insurance program that would guide all future legislation in which it reiterated the five points of the Lenin program: (1) all workers and all of the city and village poor would be covered; (2) it would include all risks of loss of income; (3) all costs would be borne by the employer; (4) unemployment and disability benefits would be equal to wages; and (5) full control of its administration would be in the hands of the insured. This communiqué was supposed to be a declaration of intent that would guide legislative action. As one would expect, however, the legislative action that followed was a clear compromise between what Lenin and the Bolsheviks wanted, and what the objective conditions of Russia at that time permitted.

Within that declaration of intent, three aspects merit special attention: (1) comprehensiveness of benefits, (b) funding by employers, and (c) administration by the insured. In terms of *comprehensiveness of the benefits*, the most important changes that took place in the short legislative period from 1917–1921 (primarily in the acts of December 11 and 29 of 1917) were aimed at expanding the coverage of benefits to include free medical care, sickness and disability insurance, and maternity benefits to all wage earners, and also at making those benefits available regardless of the period of enrollment of the beneficiary and regardless of his or her wage. Cash benefits and pensions were weighted according to the average wage in a locality rather than the previous earnings of the beneficiary. Reflecting the nature of those changes of policy, a later decree of October 31, 1918 spoke of *social security* instead of *social insurance*. However, the degree to which those ambitious programs were implemented in those times of great economic scarcity is highly questionable.[5]

Regarding *administration of the social security scheme*, the initial legislation (December 19, 1917) provided for a completely decentralized system of local funds administered by representatives of the insured and of the trade unions. And as to the funding, the benefits were to be paid by the employer according to a policy that could best be defined in today's terms as one of "soaking the rich." Also, to complement those funds, the central government repeatedly ordered that nationalized property be turned over to local insurance funds to enable them to make payments, at least in kind.

Events that took place after the enactment of that initial legislation forced changes in both the administration as well as the funding of the social security system, including health services. The very profound changes in the patterns of ownership of the economy that took place during the period 1918-1920 were frequently greater and in many cases faster than the Bolshevik leadership wanted. As Rimlinger indicates, to a large degree the Bolsheviks legalized what was already taking place, most often quite spontaneously.[6] This was particularly the case with the acquisition of land by the landless peasantry, and with the take-over of factories by the industrial working class. As Trotsky wrote, "The masses showed themselves to be a hundred times to the left of the leftest party."[7] Actually, available evidence seems to indicate that the leadership neither intended nor felt comfortable with such massive changes in the relations of property in such a short period of time. To add to the problems facing the Bolshevik leadership, the strict economic blockade established against Soviet Russia by the Allies threatened to strangulate the nascent Bolshevik regime. The result of these two objective conditions was that industrial production in 1920 declined to 13 percent of the 1913 level.[8]

These rapid and uncontrollable events profoundly affected the implementation and enactment of the Bolshevik health and social security programs. The class of employers that was to be a main contributor to the funding of social security was disappearing very rapidly indeed, with the state taking over far larger parts of funding than was originally envisioned or planned. Also, the increased centralization of the direction of economic production thought to be necessary to avoid economic chaos required stronger central direction of social policy, with the central government taking direct responsibility for administering the social security programs, and with the previously-established executive committees of the local funds losing their executive functions and retaining merely advisory ones.

Deprofessionalization and Democratization of the Health Sector

The initial steps after the October Revolution in the health sector were focused upon enlarging and redistributing the numbers and types of resources. More and better distribution was the motto. Prior to the October Revolution, the health sector was aimed primarily at serving the urban areas and the nobility and upper-middle classes, and to a far smaller degree the rural areas through the

Zemstvo medical program. Within that scheme, the majority of medical practice fell under the rubric of liberal medicine. In the candid words of the Russian writer, Versayev, a physician himself: "Medicine is a science dealing with the treatment of the rich only. In relation to everybody else, it is merely a theoretical science dealing with how they could be cured if they were rich."[9]

In this process of redefinition of priorities in the health sector, a clear conflict appeared between the Bolshevik Party and the majority of the medical profession, represented by the Pirogov Society. They represented different interests, visions, and understandings of what health services should be and do. The medical profession, petit bourgeois in class extraction, had supported the Provisional Government of Kerensky. It wanted an autonomous national health service run by the medical profession with payment for the services of its members either from local insurance funds or from private sources. On the other hand, the Bolsheviks favored administration of the health services by the local Soviets of peasants and workers—local authorities elected by all wage earners, including salaried workers, peasants, and soldiers—and a salary payment to the professions, as for any other workers. It is interesting to note that, at that time, the Webbs in England, also with dramatic opposition from the British Medical Association, were calling for the running of the health services by the local authorities and payment for those services via a salary arrangement. A third characteristic of Bolshevik policies at the beginning of the October Revolution was the insistence that while the entire health sector should be run by the local Soviets, each health institution within a Soviet should be run by committees elected by those working in the institutions.

Not surprisingly, the Pirogov Society objected to the Bolshevik program since its implementation would have led to serious curtailment of both the class and professional interests of its members. As to the former, the Pirogov Society felt that the Bolshevik program was biased, as it undoubtedly was, in favor of the working class and against the bourgeoisie, the class to which it belonged. Professionally, the Society felt that it would lose its dominant position over the decision-making process in the health sector (as it undoubtedly would) should the Bolshevik policies be implemented. Consequently, the Pirogov Society joined the Menshevik and other parties in a campaign of opposition to and sabotage of the implementation of the Bolshevik program.

American scholars, among them Mark Field, question this sabotage, since they assume that sabotage by the medical profession would have gone "against the traditional sense of social duty and professional ethics, which makes the alleged refusal to help wounded men difficult to believe."[10] Instead, Field postulates that there was no sabotage and that such prefabricated allegations against the medical association were used by the Bolsheviks in order to dissolve the Pirogov Society. This historical interpretation, however, assumes that the medical profession, having to choose between idealism (the ethical values of medicine) or materialism (the economic interests of physicians), would choose the former over the latter. This assumption lacks historical validity. Actually, the implementation of the Bolshevik program did dramatically affect the material conditions (class and professional interests) of the medical profession. To assume that the medical profession would not rebel by all available means, including sabotage, against that dramatic curtailment of benefits because of a response to a higher call, is an idealistic interpretation of history in general and of the history of the medical profession in particular, and is to ignore all historical evidence. Indeed, a long series of historical events—the most recent occurring during the Allende government in Chile where the Chilean Medical Association did sabotage the government policies which it perceived as curtailing its interests and supported, by all available means, a military coup against that government—shows quite clearly that for the majority of the medical profession, when having to choose between the defense of its privileges and the Hippocratic oath, the choice is quite clear.[11]

In dispute in the conflict between the medical association and the Bolshevik Party were two substantial class interests, those of the bourgeoisie versus those of the working class, which meant also a substantial conflict between two interpretations of the functions of the health sector. The victory of one was difficult without the curtailment of the other.

In this conflict between the medical association and the Bolshevik government, the role played by other groups in the health labor force and their unions was of paramount importance. Prior to the October Revolution and back in the early years of this century, there had been a large movement for unionization among health workers. Among the first groups to be unionized were the feldshers and lower-rank hospital personnel. Both unions were close to the Bolshevik Party and constituted the most radical among the health workers' unions. Another was the nurses' union, with a large membership of 18,000 nurses. Even physicians and pharmacists unionized to defend their interests. By the time of the October Revolution, practically all medical professionals and workers were members of independently working unions. It was perceived by most unions as imperative after the October Revolution that all unions in the health sector be amalgamated into a single health workers' union. With the feldshers' union (composed largely of army feldshers) as the driving force, a movement to unite into one single union developed that in 1920 culminated in the overall integration of all unions, including the physicians' union, into the all-Russian Central Council of Trade Unions.[d] Reflecting the fact that the majority of health workers were women, the membership of the union was approximately 60 percent female.[12] The objectives of the union, as perceived by its leadership, were (1) to support improvements in the knowledge and skills of the health labor force, (2) to be responsible for the production and distribution of all human health resources, and (3) to share the control of the health institutions with the local Soviets.

---

[d]The physicians' union was the last to accept its overall integration into a single union.

It is interesting to note that the Bolshevik Party relied very heavily on the health workers' union to counter the power of the medical association. By giving increasing power to that union at the expense of the Pirogov Society, the party shifted the basis of power among health workers from the majority of the physicians to the majority of health workers, including the Bolshevik physicians represented in the health workers' unions.[e] Moreover, the final dissolution of the Pirogov Society and the later integration of the physicians' union into the overall health workers' union served to deprofessionalize the medical profession. Instead of being divided into sections according to specialties as the professional society had been, the union was divided into sections according to subjects of endeavor of the health workers: (1) scientific research and teaching, (2) urban medicine, (3) rural medicine, (4) veterinary work, (5) railways, (6) pharmaceuticals, (7) army and navy, and (8) mining and workshop medicine.

Here, it is interesting to note the difference in strategy between Lenin's Bolshevik Party in the Soviet Union and Bevan's Labour Party in Great Britain in their dealings and relationships with the medical profession during the creation of the socialist health services in the USSR and of the British National Health Service (NHS). In his strategy, Bevan questioned neither the professionalism and class interests of the profession nor the class structure of Great Britain in 1948. For him, the integration of the medical profession and its cooptation within the NHS was primarily a management question. Thus, he dealt with the most powerful agents of the medical profession—the Royal Colleges and the British Medical Association (BMA)—in order to establish a compromise that would allow collaboration between the medical profession and the NHS while respecting, maintaining, and even strengthening the professional and class interests of the Royal Colleges and the BMA. In this bargaining process, Bevan dismissed the Socialist Medical Association, the radical group within the profession, as an inconsequential group of no importance. Lenin's strategy, to the contrary, did question the professional and class interests of the medical profession as well as the prevalent class structure of Russia at that time, a class structure that was also replicated in the health sector. Thus, his government's strategy was to deliberately weaken the Pirogov Society and shift the power within the labor force in the health sector to the majority of workers in that sector, to the unions, and to the socialist physicians. Thus, in restructuring the health sector, the Bolsheviks encouraged the development of all workers' unions as a force to counterbalance the power of the medical profession. For Lenin, the strategy towards the medical profession was not a managerial strategy but a political one of deprofessionalization and democratization of the health sector. These different strategies are of paramount

---

[e]Although the health workers' union did not include the physicians' union in the period 1917-1920, it did include individual physicians supportive of the Bolshevik government.

importance in understanding the subsequent events in both the Soviet Union and those occurring in the development of the British National Health Service.

Centralization Versus Decentralization in the Health Sector: Workers' Control, Soviet Power, and State Control

With the advent of the October Revolution, the spontaneous takeovers of land, factories, and social institutions (e.g., banks and hospitals) by peasants and industrial and social workers gained momentum. In the health sector, institutions were taken over by workers who established health workers' committees[f] similar both in composition and responsibility to the industrial workers' committees in the factories.[13] Committee members were elected by the workers of the institutions and had as their responsibility the political and administrative direction of the institutions. Those takeovers, encouraged and stimulated by the Bolsheviks prior to the October Revolution, created some concern and uneasiness among both the unions as well as some sectors of the Bolshevik Party, primarily those sectors led by Lenin, after the revolution. Indeed, the expression "Power to the workers" was interpreted variously by different groups, each one claiming to be representative of the workers' interests. The spontaneous takeovers of factories and social institutions like hospitals that continued after the October Revolution were primarily encouraged by the left wing of the Bolshevik Party, and the anarcho-syndicalist groups, referred to by Lenin as ultraleft syndicalism,[14] which wanted the direct control of the factories and the institutions by the producers working in those institutions. Those workers' committees elected regional and national committees, establishing a power parallel to and usually in conflict with the power of the Soviets. In opposition to that understanding of "Power to the workers" was the health workers' union, whose program, as mentioned before, included the direction of all health institutions as well as of the mechanisms of regulation and control of all human resources in the health sector. The health workers' unions wanted to run the hospitals through committees appointed by the union leadership.

In opposition to the ultraleft syndicalists and also to the unions, the Leninists in the Bolshevik Party wanted the health institutions to be directed by the local Soviets, the key administrative authorities of the nascent Soviet state. Those Soviets were the "organs of the state power in territories, regions, autonomous regions, areas, districts, cities, and rural localities."[15] They were elected by workers, peasants, and soldiers, including also professionals and intellectuals. Those that "employed others for the sake of profit," "those who live on income not arising from their own labor," "private businessmen," "monks and priests,"

---

[f]Prior to the October Revolution, the hospitals were administered by medical directors appointed either by the central or by the Zemstvo governments.

and "criminals and imbeciles" were not allowed to vote for the Soviets (limitations that were dropped in 1936). The local Soviets (urban and rural) were to elect the regional Soviets and these would elect the All-Union Soviets.[g] It is also worth emphasizing that in order to strengthen the weight of the industrial working class and that of the urban centers over the peasantry in rural areas, the All-Union Soviets were elected on the basis of proportional representation, in which the number of delegates to that All-Union Soviet was affixed at one delegate for every 25,000 electors in the urban areas and one for every 125,000 electors in the rural areas. Thus the urban-based industrial workers were given greater electoral strength than the rural-based peasantry.[h] The Party program of 1919 clearly stated that "our soviet constitution reflects the leading role of the urban worker in the revolution by retaining a certain preference for the industrial proletariat."[16]

Within that structure, each Soviet had a health committee or commissariat that was responsible for both the policy and administrative direction of the health sector in its administrative unit. This Leninist vision and the implied structure of the state conflicted with the left-wing opposition that wanted the health institutions to be operated by health workers' committees in collaboration with and under the guidance of the factory workers' committees. The Leninists, having supported workers' control at the beginning of the October Revolution, increasingly felt that in the final analysis the control of factories and social institutions by factory and institutional workers' committees was incompatible with the creation of any planning policy to end what they considered the anarchy of production. Confusion then existed as to what the Party's policies toward workers' control should be. As one of the leaders of that Party candidly indicated: "If one asks oneself how our Party before the 25th of October conceived the system of workers' control as a whole and on the basis of what economic order we meant to construct it, we shall nowhere find a clear answer."[17]

It was not until 1920 that the Bolshevik Party, renamed the Communist Party in 1918, established the main elements of the state structure in which the management and administration of the productive units and social institutions (e.g., hospitals) would be assumed by the local Soviets. Specifically, the health institutions would be run by the local Soviets in which representatives of the health workers were a very small minority. Each institution would have a director appointed by the local Soviet, with an advisory body elected by workers of

---

[g]The 1936 reforms called for the direct election of all Soviets by voters in the respective administrative units.

[h]It was felt by the Party that the higher class consciousness of the urban workers and their greater effectiveness against the bourgeoisie entitled them to a privileged franchise in the revolutionary state.

that institution. The role of that body, however, would be only advisory, with executive power remaining with the Soviets. Not unexpectedly, this Leninist strategy was opposed by the workers' factory committees which wanted direct election of the executive committees of the institutions by the workers of those institutions, and by the unions who wanted those institutions run by union-appointed executive committees.[18]

The decision to delegate authority to the local Soviets as opposed to giving maximum authority to the central government was made partly because of the great uneasiness and even hostility that the leadership of the Bolshevik Party felt toward the state bureaucracy. It perceived that the majority of civil servants (those on the top) were members of either the nobility or petite bourgeoisie, and as such, hostile to Bolshevik programs. After the October Revolution, the state machinery remained not only intact but largely in the hands of its original personnel. As Lenin had indicated:

We have an undetermined number of Party militants at the higher levels—at the least a few thousands, at most ten thousand. However, at the base of that hierarchy, hundreds of thousands of ex-functionaries whom we inherited from the Czar and the bourgeoisie, are working, partly consciously and partly unconsciously, against us.[19]

Moreover, total centralization of power in the social sphere could have meant an increase of power to that state apparatus despite the Party's goal to destroy the state machinery. The only difference within the Party at that time was with respect to the speed with which that machinery should be dissolved.[20]

However, objective conditions in Russia during the period 1918-1920—i.e., a civil war in which the majority of Russian land was controlled by the White Russians assisted by the Allies, the economic blockade declared against the Bolshevik government by most European countries, and a condition of spontaneous takeovers of both industry and land—seriously affected both industrial and agricultural production and had quite an impact on the Soviet economy. Those economic conditions forced a reappraisal of initial Bolshevik policies, a reappraisal that was resolved towards increased centralization in the political, economic, and social policies of the Party. Politically, that centralization meant increased control by the Party over all organs of the state. And in the economic and social areas, it meant (1) intensified centralization of the direction of economic production (primarily of heavy industry); (2) an increase in the trend towards collectivization of land with the establishment of state farms; and (3) greater centralization of policy in the social sectors, with centralization of the administration of social insurance and increased centralization of the normative and regulative functions in the health sector by the Central People's Commissariat of Health, established in 1918 under the directorship of Dr. Semaschko, who had been a constant companion of Lenin's, in both Paris and Geneva, during Lenin's exile. It was not until later, however, in the Constitution of 1928 that the Commissariat was given the right to direct the normative and regulatory functions of the health sector.

Also at that time, and in addition to the centralization of those normative and regulatory functions, the Central People's Commissariat of Health was assigned active responsibility for the control of epidemics (primarily typhus, cholera, and dysentery) that were rampant in the USSR and that constituted a threat to the survival of the Soviet system far greater than that represented by the White Armies or the economic blockade.[21] As Lenin said, "Either socialism will defeat the louse, or the louse will defeat socialism."[22]

The Health Labor Force in the Soviet Union in the Period 1917-1921

The initial period of the Soviet Revolution had more impact on the size than on the nature of the health labor force. In terms of physicians, for five years medical education continued to follow the traditional German model that, as previously indicated, reflected a mechanistic understanding of medicine. In that respect, the immediate effect of the Soviet Revolution was not to question the meaning of medicine and thus the medical curriculum (the issue was not even raised), but to increase the number of physicians to compensate for the high number of casualties among those who fought in the Red Army. As Semaschko states, not a single physician survived the epidemics plaguing the eastern regions of Russia.[23] Responding to that demand for physicians, the number of medical students increased dramatically, resulting in an increase in the overall number of physicians from 22,000 in 1917 to 63,162 in 1928.[24]

Besides this large increase in the production of physicians, the most important changes that took place in that period of Soviet history were in the class and sex composition of the medical student body.[25] Prior to the Soviet Revolution, women composed less than 10 percent of all medical students, and even then, they could only attend special medical schools, the most important of which was the women's medical school in St. Petersburg. Similarly, Jews were allotted a special quota of no more than 3 percent of total enrollment. In contrast to that situation, the Soviet Revolution made a commitment to open the university to both sexes and all classes and races previously discriminated against, and in medical and all other schools preference was given to applicants from the working class and peasantry, as well as to women. Moreover, to facilitate the incorporation of workers into academic training, special workers' schools and faculties, or rabyaks, were established, designed to prepare adult workers for higher educational institutions. Under that program,

If a laborer who had been working for at least three years in industry wanted to study medicine . . . he was admitted to a Medical Workers' Faculty. There, while still working in the factory, he would be instructed during a three- or four-years' course in language, literature, mathematics, physics, chemistry, and political science, so that he might meet the entrance requirements of the medical school.[26]

It is interesting to note that the aim of those programs was to increase the availability of medical and university education to workers without altering the essential character of that education. Thus, the conceptual modes of medicine remained intact. Actually, this lack of change in the conceptual components of medicine, at least in the initial stages of the Soviet Revolution, is more typical than atypical of the early stages of socialist revolutions. In both China and Cuba, for example, while a very dramatic redistribution of resources took place in the initial years of those revolutions, the nature and type of those resources did not change, e.g., the content of the medical curriculum remained unaltered. It was in subsequent years—thirty years in China (under the Cultural Revolution) and ten years in Cuba (in the 1971 university reforms) after the starting date of the revolution—that profound changes were made not only in expanding but also in redefining the nature of those resources.

The resolution of the previously-mentioned conflict between the Pirogov Society (representing the medical profession) and the Bolshevik government in favor of the latter, and the subsequent deprofessionalization and unionization of the medical profession, went hand in hand with the shift from liberal fee-for-service medicine to the socialized salary-based method of remuneration. And although private practice was never forbidden by the Bolshevik government, the poor economic conditions of Russia at the beginning of the Soviet Revolution and the rapid disappearance of the nobility and upper-middle class effected a rapid dissolution of clientele for private medicine. Thus, the majority of physicians were employed by the local Soviets and paid a basic salary augmented by a special tariff for added services. The basic salaries were approximately 180 to 250 rubles per month, and approximately 10 percent of physicians worked with the Red Army.[27]

The absence of a central regulatory mechanism, as well as the incipient and somewhat chaotic formation of the local Soviets side by side with the wide disparity in development of urban and rural areas, explains the absence of a profound redistribution of human resources among the different regions of Soviet Russia during the first periods of the October Revolution. And although there was indeed a redistributive effect among social classes, at least with respect to the availability of human resources, that effect took place primarily within and not across regions.

Lenin and Kautsky's Interpretations of the State and Their Implications for Medicine

Because of the importance of Lenin's thought in the creation of the Soviet system which included social security and medicine, let me expand on Lenin's ideas of the state, of which these two activities were part and parcel. And the first thing that has to be said is that Lenin, although far from the consistent and infallible strategist that some of his uncritical supporters claim (as I will later illustrate in Chapter 10), greatly contributed to the understanding of the nature of political power and the state.[i] His major work on this subject is *State and Revolution*, written in 1917 in response and as a rebuttal to Kautsky's interpretation of the state and his alternative strategy for revolutionary change. Due to the importance of both theories in the understanding of a socialist strategy in the health sector, let me first summarize them and later I will outline the unexplored implications of those strategies for medicine.

Kautsky's strategy called for a seizure of power. He indicated that what "is essential is purely and simply to take possession of the state machine which is already there, and to use it for one's own ends."[28] Consequently, he advocated the seizure of state power by a minority which was supposed to be representative of the working class, and which would use the state bureaucracy to govern on behalf of the working class. The state machinery or bureaucracy, however, was not to be destroyed or changed "because bureaucracy, i.e., the difference between governors and governed, cannot be suppressed and will always survive."[29] In other words, according to Kautsky, the revolution was the transfer of state power from one class to another.

Lenin, however, felt that the seizure of state power had to be accompanied by the change, dilution, and even destruction of the state machinery. And this implied far more than taking over the Winter Palace or the Department of the Interior. Lenin's strategy meant the revolutionary change of all state institutions, with the dissolution of the state bureaucracy, and then finally, of the distinction between governors and the governed.

Indeed, according to Lenin, the state structure (including the bureaucracy), which was inherited from the nobility and the old order, could not be used to serve the new socialist order. He felt that the pattern of relations prevalent in the feudal and capitalist orders was replicated in the state machinery, and that unless that machinery disappeared, the old order would be reestablished. Thus, it was Lenin's strategy (the Lenin of *State and Revolution*) to gradually substitute the state machinery's power to another type of power in which the population would take direct control of the government. This change would not take place overnight, but rather, it would be a gradual process with the increased takeover of the still existent state by the self-governing population. Accordingly, "In socialism, the mass of the population will rise to take an independent part, not only in voting and elections, but also in the everyday administration of the state."[30] In that respect, the socialist revolution for Lenin was more than the transfer of state power from one class to another.

---

[i]The term "state" is used here to refer to all branches of the government and its administration, including the executive, legislative, and judicial branches, the armed forces, and activities run by the government such as social and health services.

It was also the passage from one type of power to another. In Lenin's words, "It was the gigantic replacement of certain institutions by other institutions of a fundamentally different order."[31] In summary, it was the redefinition of power altogether.

At the political level, Lenin's strategy for change meant the change from parliamentarianism to Soviet power with the local Soviets being the primary agencies of self-government, the direct government not only for but by the community of producers. It is worth underlining that Lenin also indicated that the change toward democratization and self-government was a step that should start from the very first day of the seizure of state power. He felt that any delays in this process would imply the mere substitution of the old masters with the new ones, however representative these new ones might be.

But that Leninist theoretical construct had to be matched with the practical realities of the Soviet Union in the early 1920s. Indeed, history is not only the result of subjective factors—including ideologies—but of objective conditions as well—i.e., the state of the material conditions of development. Thus, Leninist theories had to be adapted to the objective conditions that determined the New Economic Policy (NEP).

These two different strategies held by Lenin and Kautsky were also present in the strategies for change in the health sector in 1917, and, I may add, also exist today in a modified version. According to the Kautskyan strategy, the actual issue in the strategy for change called for the control of that sector by the state. Consequently, for those strategists (and, as I will illustrate in subsequent sections, that includes Stalinists to social democrats), the socialization of medicine was its nationalization and state control by parties that hopefully represented the working class.

According to the Leninist interpretation of change, however, the actual strategical issue was not only the transfer of the control over medicine from one class to another, but was also the passage from one type of medicine to another. In other words, the Leninist strategy was not only the one that changed the quantity and distribution of medical resources, but changed the nature of medicine as well. In that respect, revolutionary medicine meant then, as it would mean today, the democratization and deprofessionalization of medicine in which the content and practice of medicine was not defined by the Party member, the bureaucrat or the expert, but by the collectivity of the population.

Needless to say that, according to that interpretation, to the same degree that the state cannot disappear overnight and there has to be a gradual dilution of the state, similarly, hierarchical, professionalized, and bureaucratized medicine cannot disappear overnight after the seizure of power. But it is of utmost importance that the trend within a socialist revolution be toward the democratization and deprofessionalization of medicine, not vice versa. Indeed, to see the socialization of medicine as the mere Kautskyan redistribution of medicine—the issue of equity—is to have a narrow, limiting, and limited understanding of socialism. But more than that, it is to allow the perpetuation of bourgeois and bureaucratic medicine with all that this implies, as will be seen in the following sections which discuss the evolution of Soviet medicine.

In summary, the experiences of the first years of the Soviet Revolution (experiences replicated, incidentally, in other socialist revolutions, as I will illustrate in the final chapter) seem to point to the following conclusions.

First, a socialist process in medicine is not the change of the control over medicine from one party to another or from one minority to another, but most importantly, the process whereby the concept and meaning of medicine change as well, i.e., from the bourgeois, individualist understanding of medicine to the collective, political, and mass understanding of medicine, resultant from massive popular participation in the decision-making and implementation of whatever form of medicine may evolve in a socialist society. Indeed, as I will later illustrate, Allende's Chile and the Chinese Cultural Revolutionary processes showed not only how the distribution but also the understanding of medicine changed when the population took direct control of their health institutions. As the Soviet period 1917–1921 clearly showed, the socialization of medicine was not only the nationalization of medicine, but most importantly, its democratization and deprofessionalization.

Second, another conclusion to be drawn from that initial experience of the October Revolution period is that a socialist process in medicine is not possible unless it is part and parcel of the larger process of the democratization of the entire society. It requires and determines politicization and class consciousness of the majority of the population to be willing to take over the direct control of its own institutions. In that respect, the period just described (as other socialist revolutionaries have also shown) shows how a socialist movement in medicine cannot exist independently of an overall socialist movement. To think otherwise is to assume an independence and autonomy in the health sector that is both unhistorical and unempirical. However, before further discussing the experience of that period (1917–1921), let us proceed with our analysis of the Soviet process. And once we have studied the subsequent stages of the Soviet Union's development, we can further develop (in the final chapter) the points which have been summarized here.

3

The New Economic Policy: 1921-1928

The Political and Economic Meaning of the New Economic Policy

War Communism, also referred to as Instant Communism, proved to be disastrous for the Russian economy.[1] In order to understand this, one has to realize that in addition to the objective conditions posed by the economic blockade and civil war, which created great constraints on the Soviet economy, there were spontaneous takeovers by factory workers and peasants that converted the incipient monopolistic and capitalist economy of pre-Soviet Russia into an economy of uncoordinated and independent multiple-producing units, much different from the economic form envisioned by the Bolsheviks. Prior to the October Revolution, Lenin had advocated an intermediate stage of state capitalism in which privately-owned monopolies would be supported, guided, and directed by the state until that historical moment when, due to the evolution and maturation of the forces of production (including the working class), the working class would take over those monopolies, creating state socialism. Subsequently, the state was to disappear altogether, giving way to communism. Instead, the events, from 1918 to 1922, made the creation of state capitalism impossible as envisioned by Lenin. Those events had the effect of breaking the economic power of the feudal landowner, the nobility, and bourgeoisie without establishing the basis for a socialist economy. In the face of this situation, the Bolshevik leadership did not have a revolutionary blueprint that could guide its policies. As Lenin candidly recognized:

We have knowledge of socialism, but as for knowledge of organization on a scale of millions, knowledge of the organization and distribution of commodities—that we have not. This the old Bolshevik leaders did not teach us . . . Nothing has been written about this yet in Bolshevik textbooks, and there is nothing in Menshevik textbooks either.[2]

The end of the civil war in 1920 created a moment of relaxation that also allowed the expression of serious discontent by the peasantry as well as by some sections of workers towards the Bolshevik government. In 1921, for example, there was a revolt of soldiers and peasants demanding direct ownership of the land by the peasantry. The peasantry, who had sided with the Red Army against the White Army, had not been satisfied with the agricultural policies of the Bolsheviks, and the hoarding and storing of food had created serious shortages in the urban areas.

31

Against this background, in March of 1921, the Tenth Congress of the Communist Party established the New Economic Policy (NEP), which implied a step toward the liberalization of the Soviet economy and its opening to the laws of the market.[3] In agriculture (the main focus of NEP), the new policy meant not the denationalization of the land, but rather the lease of state land to private owners and peasants, with agricultural production following the free operation of the market. In this manner, the state's relation to the peasantry was that of being merely a tax collector. Moreover, the fiscal policies of the state changed to stimulate a favorable rate of return for the peasant based on his productivity; the level of taxation was related to the productivity of the cultivator, i.e., the higher his productivity, the lower the level of taxation. Furthermore, the price of agricultural products as well as industrial commodities was left to be defined by the invisible hand of the market with minimal state intervention.

In the industrial sector, the program establishing NEP encouraged the denationalization of state enterprises not considered basic to industrial development, and stimulated the independent and autonomous operation of the remaining state enterprises on a commercial basis without automatic state support. Moreover, the consumer goods sector was deliberately encouraged, with the products of those industries quickly mobilized to revitalize the market exchange between industry and agriculture, and between cities and the small towns and villages. As a result of this policy, a large number of small and local industries appeared. A 1923 census of 165,000 industrial enterprises showed that 88 percent were either in private ownership or leased to private individuals, with 8.5 percent owned by the state and 3 percent by cooperatives.[4] However, due to the very small size of those private enterprises, they employed less than 10 percent of all industrial labor and accounted for only 4.9 percent of industrial production. State industrial enterprises remained dominant in the industrial sector. The difference, a meaningful one at that, between the operation of industries during War Communism and NEP was that under NEP they were to emphasize consumer as opposed to capital goods, and operate on an independent and almost autonomous basis without regard to an overall plan, in accordance with the law of supply and demand. However, under those policies certain sectors of the industry were further encouraged and supported, such as the extractive industries and electricity. It was during this period that Lenin coined the frequently-quoted aphorism that communism was Soviet power plus electricity.

Social Security and Health Services During the New Economic Policy

Consistent with the establishment of these priorities, the comprehensiveness of social security was discontinued, covering only wage earners and excluding self-employed peasants, artisans, and professionals. Moreover, the principle of social security was modified to allow variance in the benefits received by the workers, depending on their labor history, productivity, and years of work. The benefits thus became skewed in favor of the skilled and semiskilled to the disadvantage of the unskilled, and social security was reshaped to increase the specialization and productivity of labor. In 1923, to further dramatize that aim, social security was moved from an independent social security commissariat to the Labor Commissariat. Insurance policies were to be established by that Commissariat, whose main responsibility was to increase the productivity of labor in industry.[5]

Also, as part of the NEP, a Labor Code was passed in 1922 which established the labor market as a mechanism to regulate wage levels.[6] The worker could move from factory to factory (which he could not during War Communism), and he could be fired as well. The result was that managers, both of public as well as private firms, felt free to operate according to principles of maximum profitability, keeping wages as low as legally permitted, with as few workers as possible. Unemployment increased and so did inflation.

Three characteristics of NEP had relevance in the health service: (1) marketability of goods and services, (2) priority to those services assumed to favor productivity, and (3) priority to agricultural production. In regard to the first, considerable sectors of the public health services were converted into private institutions with the provision of free services being continued only for those insured under the social security scheme, all others paying by fee at the time of service. The effects of those policies were many, but a critical one was replacement of the incipient mechanism of the Soviets' allocation of resources by the market allocation of human resources. In addition, due to the impoverished condition of large sectors of the Russian population, many physicians could not start a practice that would enable them to survive in the private sector. Semaschko mentions that in 1923, Moscow had 956 doctors registered with the Labor Office as unemployed.[7] The second characteristic had the effect of giving the highest priority to occupational and industrial health services with emphasis on extractive industries, such as mining. With respect to the third characteristic, at the Twelfth Meeting of the Communist Party in 1925, the decision was made to implement a structure of rural health services following local governmental divisions. Basically, that structure consisted of small medical divisions called uchastocks (physicians' sections), which were part of a rayon (district), with several rayons forming an oblast. In this structure, primary care services could be provided in the uchastock, secondary and hospital care services in the rayon, and further specialized services would be provided in the oblast. The initial regionalization of services was established at that time. Physicians graduating after 1925 were sent to staff those centers as partial repayment for their state-supported education. It is interesting to note that to make the physicians' lives more attractive, the local Soviets were supposed to provide housing and transportation facilities. In addition, responding to the priorities given in NEP to agricultural production and the peasantry, there was during this time the creation of preventive and sanitation stations operated by the local Soviets, as was true for most health services. The responsibilities of these sanitation stations were to prevent contamination of water, air, soil, and food.

4

The Period of Industrialization: 1928-1953

The Political Determinants of Industrialization

When the Bolsheviks took power in 1917, Lenin and the entire leadership in the Party felt that socialism could not take place in one country alone. Also, they believed that the European working class was ripe for taking over the different bourgeois governments existing in Europe at that time. Actually, and contrary to what is customarily believed, this theory of the impossibility of socialism in one country was held not only by Trotsky[1] (the supposed holder of that theory), but also by Lenin and Stalin, among others. Indeed, Stalin had written in his *Foundations of Leninism* (April 1924) that "overthrowing the power of the bourgeoisie and establishing the power of the proletariat in a single country does not yet guarantee the complete victory of socialism ... The victory of socialism requires the victory of the revolution in several countries."[2]

However, the absence of revolutionary uprisings by the working classes in those European countries and their failure to come to the defense of the nascent Soviet Revolution,[a] as well as the establishment of a strong economic blockade against the Soviet Union in which most of the Western countries participated, created a new situation which prompted the Bolshevik leadership to develop on its own, i.e., to catch up with the societies of Western Europe whose dominant classes were profoundly hostile to the Bolshevik regime. As Stalin indicated in February 1931,

If we do not want our socialist fatherland defeated and its independence lost ... we must eliminate its backwardness in the shortest time possible and beat a real Bolshevik tempo toward the establishment of a socialist economy. There is no other way. In this connection Lenin himself said that either we perish or we overcome the advanced capitalist societies. We are behind the capitalist countries by fifty to a hundred years. But we must catch up with them in ten years. Either we bring this about or we are finished.[3]

Socialism was now possible in one country, but not in a backward one. In contrast to his position in 1924, Stalin indicated in 1926 that "socialism was possible ... to be built in our society, with the sympathy and support of

---

[a]Important in explaining this lack of working class uprisings were the nationalistic views of the Western European social democratic parties (heavily influenced by the German Social Democratic Party), which instead of struggling against the bourgeois governments (as did the Bolsheviks), supported these governments during World War I and thereafter.

the workers of other countries, but without the preliminary victory of the proletarian revolution in other countries. . ."[4] That edifice of socialism, however, could not be built in the backward Soviet Union of that time. Primitive capital accumulation was needed which would allow the development of socialism at a later stage. The first and foremost task was to develop the "forces of production," by which were meant primarily sciences, technology, machines, productivity, skills, etc., that would allow such economic development.[5] In that process, industrialization, economic management, science, and technology were to be the main determinants of progress. As perceived by all currents within the Party, from Bakunin on the right to Stalin in the center to Trotsky on the left, the main political task at the time was to stimulate, guide, and produce capital accumulation that would enable them to develop the economy to such a level that socialism would follow automatically. As Trotsky had said: "The strength and stability of regimes is defined in the last analysis by the relative productivity of labor. A socialist economy on the way to surpassing capitalism technically would be assured of a socialist development almost automatically."[6] The first task of the Party, then, was to build the material bases that would enable the continuation of socialism at a later stage. First and foremost was the development of capital, i.e., the process of primitive capital accumulation.

While agreeing on this goal of capital accumulation, there was less agreement on how to achieve it. The group that historically has been referred to as the right wing of the Party, led by Bakunin, felt that capital accumulation should take place primarily through a gradual process of industrialization. It suggested leaving most light industry, trade, services (including medical services), and agriculture in the private sector. The state sector (including heavy industry, which should be operated according to criteria of profitability) would direct the rest of the economy through fiscal policies. Thus, the right-wing position was basically that of a continuation of NEP.

The Trotskyist current, the left of the Party, believed that capital accumulation and industrialization should be forced, and based on the complete nationalization and state ownership and direction of both industrial and agricultural production. Stalin, at that time, took a center position. After Lenin died in 1924, Stalin and his faction, the most important within the Party, took Trotsky's position while excluding him from the Party and then exiling him.

Trotsky's policies, later to become Stalin's policies, stated that necessary industrialization was to be based on the capital accumulated from (1) the savings resultant from squeezing the peasantry, i.e., the peasantry would give more in value to the industrial sector than it in turn would receive, and the difference would be used for investment; and (2) the savings from the working class, keeping the level of consumption very low as compared to the level of production. This strategy would have, as its main components, (1) rapid industrialization, and (2) collectivization of agriculture. The implementation of those two policies would also require a third condition, centralized political control.

After Lenin's death in 1924, and following a period of internal struggle from which Stalin emerged victorious, the first five-year plan (1928) incorporated most of Trotsky's policies. Actually, it is paradoxical, to say the least, that current proponents of Trotskyism bitterly criticize Stalin's economic policies, usually referred to as economic Stalinism, when Stalin did adopt and implement a program that basically coincided with Trotsky's policies. As Deutscher, one of the few Trotskyists who was aware of the paradox, writes,

. . . at a stroke, the dilemmas [of Trotsky's group] were immensely aggravated. It became almost ludicrous for its members to chew over old slogans, to clamour for more industrialization, to protest against the appeasement of rural capitalism. . . . [Trotsky's group] either had to admit that Stalin was doing its job for it or it had to re-equip itself and 'rearm' politically for any further struggle. Trotsky, Rakovsky, and others were indeed working to bring the Opposition's ideas up to date. But events moved faster than even the most quick-minded of theorists.[7]

Due to the great importance of industrialization, agricultural collectivization, and political centralization in explaining the evolution of social security and of the health sector, not only during the period 1928-1953 but even today, let me expand on each one of those policies.

Industrialization

The results of the commitment to industrialization presented in the first five-year plans (1928-1933, 1933-1938, and subsequent ones) of the Soviet Union were most impressive. The average annual growth in the period 1928-1940 was between 17.5 and 20.3 percent, and the overall industrial output in the Soviet Union rose from 6.9 percent of the overall U.S. industrial output in 1928, to 45.1 percent in 1938.[8] Actually, whereas it took the U.S. one-hundred years to increase its heavy industry output from 18.2 percent to 55.8 percent of total industrial production, the Soviet Union achieved a more impressive increase from 39.5 percent to 73.1 percent in only 33 years.[9] Such a rapid industrial growth was based on (1) capital-intensive as opposed to labor-intensive investments;[10] (2) nationalization and central direction of all industry, e.g., gross industrial production in the private sector fell from 18.7 percent of the output in 1924-1925 to 0.03 percent in 1938;[11] and (3) a policy of optimizing production and minimizing consumption. Since much has been written about the low rate of growth of consumption in the USSR, it is important to emphasize that while the rate of household consumption actually declined from 1928 to 1940 in the Soviet Union, during 1940-1950 it underwent a higher increase than in the United States for the same period. Over the period 1928-1955, Soviet household consumption increased by 1.7 percent annually, identical to the American rise between 1929 and 1957, although overall consumption was far higher in the United States.[12]

That process of rapid industrialization determined a large growth in the non-agricultural work force, increasing from 10 to 45 million between 1926 and 1955. As Aron indicates, in the United States it took twice as long (1880-1930) to achieve a similar growth rate.[13] Parallel to that expansion in numbers, there was also a change in the sex composition of the Soviet labor force. The percentage of women in the labor force increased from 30 percent in 1928 to 40 percent in 1940, and as a result of World War II, rose to 70 percent in 1942. After the war the percentage declined to 45 percent, which is still quite high when compared with 20 percent in Western Europe and 15 percent in the United States at the same time.[14] It is very likely that the increased involvement of women in the labor force was primarily responsible for (1) a decline in the birthrate in the USSR during the period 1928-1948, (2) a decline in the average family size (from 4.10 persons per family in 1927 to 3.80 in 1938), and (3) an increase in the ratio of productive to nonproductive members of the family.[15] The implications of those demographic changes for both social security legislation as well as for health care delivery were many, as I will discuss later.

Also as a consequence of the massive program of industrialization (as well as of the collectivization of agriculture), the Soviet Union went through a process of urbanization practically unknown in prior human history. The percentage of the Russian population living in urban areas grew from 19 percent (28.7 million people) to 33 percent (63.1 million) of the total population during the period 1929-1940.[16] Actually, according to Meissner, it took the United States thirty years (from 1900 to 1930) and Great Britain sixty years (from 1871 to 1931) to achieve an identical rate of urban growth.[17] The urban population growth in the USSR, however, was mainly due to a massive move of the population from the countryside (accounting for 82.1 percent of the growth) rather than from natural increases (representing 17.9 percent of the urban growth).[18] The massive movements from rural areas created large numbers of environmental, nutritional, and health problems that I will discuss in subsequent sections.

Collectivization of the Land

As a result of the spontaneous land seizures by the peasantry that took place in 1917 and 1918, as well as the subsequent land policies of the Bolshevik government, by the end of 1928, the year when the first five-year plan started, 96 percent of the land was owned by peasants. Because of the nature of the takeovers, however, most of the ownership was in the form of very small holdings, considered by the Bolshevik leadership to be too small to sustain food production and create the surplus considered basic to the success of industrialization. And the agricultural output from the state and collective farms stimulated by the government was minimal. Those farms covered little more than 1 percent of the cultivated area throughout the USSR, and they produced only 2 percent of the total grain crop. As a result of this system of private ownership of land, there were at the beginning of the first five-year plan three main classes in rural Russia: the kulaks or wealthy landowners, whose power and size increased during NEP; the middle peasants, with small holdings; and the majority of the farm population, the poor peasants, who either worked for the kulaks or owned small holdings considered by the Bolshevik Party to be too small to be productive.

The intention of the first five-year plan was to slowly expand the percentage of land under collective farms. It was envisioned that only 15 percent of the land would be collectivized by the end of the plan. The lack of success of that cautious, gradual collectivization, greatly attributed to the strong resistance of the kulaks, resulted in a profound change in Bolshevik agricultural policies toward a most intensive collectivization of the majority of land. Due to this policy, 93 percent of all the land was collectivized by the concluding year of the plan.[19] Never before had a country gone through such a radical change in the system of land tenure within such a short period of time. Needless to say, the kulaks opposed such nationalization since it implied their end as a class, and, for many of them, the actual end of their existence. According to Stalin himself, 10 million kulaks and peasants were either killed or died during that period in a policy of ruthless extermination of any actual or potential opponent to collectivization.[20] According to Churchill, the decision to eliminate the kulaks appears to have been the most difficult decision of Stalin's life.[21]

The massive collectivization of land created a dramatic dislocation of production, with a decline in the overall agricultural production during the period 1930-1938,[22] particularly in livestock production. In 1938, the end year of the second five-year plan, the numbers of sheep, goats, pigs, horses, and cows were below the figures for 1928, the initial year of the first plan.[b] Still, that campaign of collectivization was not without its economic successes. The overall amount of grain and other marketable products such as potatoes doubled during the period 1928-1939.[24] And most of the capital invested in the industrialization campaign was based on the forced savings of the peasantry, according to Stalin's (and Trotsky's) policy of squeezing the peasantry to allow and support industrialization and its overall objective of capital accumulation.

Centralized Political Control

The very dramatic processes of industrialization and agricultural collectivization were accompanied at the political level by a great degree of centralization of political power, power which resided in a small percentage of the higher Party echelons led by Stalin. An iron discipline was established in which diversity of

---

[b]The massive sabotage of the collectivization campaign forced some concessions in the initial form of that campaign. Peasants were allowed to own animals and small holdings of land, the products of which could be sold in the private market. Actually, three-quarters of all cows, for example, were privately owned by 1938.[23]

opinions, groupings, and factions within the Party was not allowed. Whoever disagreed with the top leadership was considered an enemy of the Soviet Revolution. In that way, according to Medvedev, a massive campaign of terror started which subjected four to five million people to repression for political reasons during the period 1936–1939, of whom "at least four to five hundred thousand of them—above all the high officials—were summarily shot; the rest were given long terms of confinement. In 1937–1938 there were days when up to a thousand people were shot in Moscow alone.[25]

Repression was especially severe toward dissenting members of the Communist Party. Acording to Medvedev, Stalin liquidated most of the old Bolsheviks, and "the NKVD arrested and killed, within two years, more Communists than had been lost in all the years of the underground struggle, the three revolutions and the Civil War."[26] As Miliband emphasizes, never has a regime killed so many Communists as did Stalin's. And among them were "many of the most dedicated and experienced cadres of foreign Communist parties in exile in the USSR."[27] Needless to say, not all of that repression was without cause. There were many elements hostile to the new Soviet order, including large numbers of elements within the state organs who employed all strategies, including sabotage, to block the Bolshevik orders. According to a survey quoted by Bettelheim, only 9 percent of the old functionaries and 13 percent of the new ones were favorable to the Soviet regime.[28] However, as Medvedev indicates, it is highly likely that the majority of the purges were motivated by the desire of the Party's top echelons to silence all dissent that the leadership perceived as capable of instigating a fissure in the overall building of industrialization. Moreover, to further facilitate the process of industrialization on the lines envisioned by the Stalinist leadership of the Party, the political authorities (1) depoliticized the direction and administration of the Soviet economy and society, with political problems becoming merely managerial ones; (2) encouraged specialization and expertise in the management of all branches of the economy; and (3) stimulated the learning and adoption of those models of development that proved to be successful in the West. It was during that period that the "expert" regained a prominent place in the state, and, as Sweezy indicates, "economics" and "not politics" was put in command.[29]

Consequent to those three commitments, substantial changes took place both in the composition of the labor force and of the Party. For example, the growth of the technical and administrative categories in the labor force, the strata in charge of administering the process of industrialization, grew from 4.6 million in 1928 to 9.6 million at the end of the second five-year plan.

Another important change that took place at this time, and which translated the great emphasis given to expertise and specialization, was the discontinuation of the policy which gave priority to members of the working class in the academic institutions. As a result of this policy, the percentage of workers and workers' children among students, which had climbed from 24.4 percent to 58 percent between 1928 and 1932, dropped to 34 percent by 1938. The percentage of students from white-collar backgrounds increased during the same period from 27.9 percent to 44 percent.[30]

Also among political changes was a revision in the composition of the Communist Party. At its Eighteenth Congress, the Party declared that it represented the Soviet people as a whole and not just the working masses. And the percentage of members from the working class, which represented 65 percent of the Party in 1939, declined to 32 percent after the war, while the percentage of technicians and administrators increased from 20 to 50 percent during the same period. It is interesting to add that this new technocracy and bureaucracy, however powerful, was ultimately subservient to the final and most powerful voice, the one of the top political structure. Indeed, the growth of that bureaucracy and technocracy was due to the need of the upper echelons of the political structure—the Party—to dominate and control the process of industrialization, not vice versa. It is important to clarify this historical note, because it has become common parlance among the "convergence theory" proponents that in both societies—the USSR and the United States—the "manager and technocrat" make up the social group which is "on the top," determining, controlling, and running the most important sectors of our economic and political institutions. As I have indicated elsewhere, this interpretation is a simplification for both societies.[31] Indeed, the dominant groups in the United States, contrary to prevalent beliefs, are not those of managers and technocrats.[32] Nor are the dominant groups in the USSR those of managers and technocrats, but rather the leadership of the political party. Managers and technocrats are servants of the political structure, not vice versa.

This specialization and hierarchicalization of labor, concomitant with the process of centralization of political power and industrialization, was further increased after World War II, with its formalization in all sectors of Soviet life, from the army (whose name changed from the Red Army of Workers and Peasants to the Armed Forces of the USSR, and which was to have as many ranks as during the Czarist times), to the university and the civil service, with the People's Commissariats explicitly re-identified as Ministries in a decree of March 15, 1946. The "Internationale," incidentally, was replaced by a national anthem.

Parallel to this re-introduction of hierarchies of labor was an increase in income differentials among those at the top and bottom. In 1928, at the beginning of the first five-year plan, the highest-paid workers were making nearly three times more than the lowest paid, and in 1940, this differential had increased to thirty times.[33]

Stalinism in Social Security and Medicine

In summary, then, Stalinism[c] was characterized by (1) dramatic industrialization

---

[c]The term "Stalinism" is used to define those characteristics of the Soviet system that emerged during Stalin's time.

and urbanization; (2) a massive campaign of agricultural collectivization, extracting the surplus needed to support industrialization; and (3) centralization of political control. These policies, in turn, determined (1) the nature and functions of social security; (2) the nature of the health sector; and (3) the production and distribution of human health resources. Allow me, then, to elaborate on these effects.

Social Security as an Enabling Factor in Industrialization

After the Fifteenth Communist Party Congress in 1927 (generally referred to as the Industrialization Congress) during which the guidelines for the first five-year plan were approved, social security was profoundly changed, first and foremost to stimulate the process of industrialization.[34] Social security was to increase the productivity and discipline of the labor force. Actually, in quite a number of measures, these changes represented a further strengthening of NEP policies. In the words of Shvernik, the Commissar of Labor:

Egalitarianism must be eradicated from social insurance. We must reconstruct the whole social insurance practice in order to give the most privileged treatment to shock workers and to those with long service. The fight against labor turnover must be put into the forefront. We shall handle social insurance as a weapon in the struggle to attach workers to their enterprises and strike hard at loafers, malingerers, and disorganizers of work ... At the center of trade-union social insurance work must be care for the worker who has been actively wrestling with the fulfillment of the industrial financial plan and the work norms.[35]

This straightforward declaration clearly established the policy directions for the social security programs. These can be analyzed in terms of what their specific objectives were and the mechanisms designed to achieve them.

First, one focus of those programs was to increase the size of the productive labor force by (1) encouraging and enabling the involvement of women in the labor force by creating a wide network of health care centers and by reducing the amount and length of maternity benefits to five weeks before and four weeks after delivery; (2) reducing and eradicating unemployment through the decree of October 9, 1930, which stopped all relief payments to the unemployed except in case of sickness or serious disability; and (3) encouraging retired workers to work by allowing them to earn their pension in addition to a regular salary or wage.

Second, the programs were aimed at reducing absenteeism and turnover of workers by (1) penalizing absenteeism, i.e., three days absence in any month was punishable by dismissal without notice;[d] (2) making social security benefits subject to the length of employment (Labor Code of 1938); (3) making the provision of some benefits, such as temporary disability benefits, equal to wages,

---

[d]Punishable absenteeisms had to be without justifiable cause, however, and the definition of "justifiable cause" was determined by labor courts and established by the unions.

subject to the labor discipline of the worker, e.g., the worker could not receive full benefits unless he had a record of at least two years of uninterrupted employment;[36] and (4) making it illegal (after 1940) for a worker to quit his job without permission from the management.[37]

Third, the type and nature of benefits provided under the social insurance programs varied depending on the sector of the labor force, with higher priority in terms of benefits given to those working in the key sectors required for fulfilling the five-year plans, e.g., iron and steel, engineering, mining, chemicals, and transportation. In line with achieving this goal of selectivity of benefits according to the sector of the labor force, the entire system of administering the social security system was changed profoundly; this function was taken away from the Commissariat of Labor in 1933 and given to different trade unions (grouped according to branch of the labor force) under the political direction of the Communist Party. The local insurance advisory boards were abolished, and local union funds appointed by the central offices of the unions were established in their place. Indeed, until 1933 the National Insurance Agency, operated by the Commissariat of Labor, appointed the local insurance advisory boards (elected by the insured) to administer the Social Security Act. However, what the Party wanted in order to meet the objectives of the five-year plan was not a governmental and administrative agency that would automatically adhere to the letter of the law, but, like the union, a structure which would be more attuned to the production and industrialization process and would be more flexible and receptive to the Party line.[38]

Industrialization and the Health Sector: Health Services as Capital Investment

Similar to social security, the health sector was to be reshaped in order to support the massive process of industrialization. A primary objective was to increase the care provided to the most productive and key sectors of the labor force. Consequently, the new call in the health sector was: "On from the struggle against epidemics to the fight for more healthy working conditions."[39] Thus, the three main developments in the health sector during this period were: (1) active development of a separate and autonomous occupational health service; (2) development of an extensive network of child care centers to enable the active involvement of women in the labor force; and (3) development of urban environmental health services to take care of the public health problems caused by the massive and unprecedented degree of urbanization which accompanied the process of industrialization.

Of the three, the most important was the development of industrial health services, which provided curative and preventive services to the worker at the working place, and whose primary objective was to reduce the widely-prevalent absenteeism and disability due to illness. According to Vladimirsky, the Commissar of Health in the late 1930s, the annual production loss due to illness in

Leningrad alone was equal to one-quarter of the yearly production in 1930, with half of those absences preventable.[40] Industrial health services were provided in industrial health centers, situated for the most part in the factories and staffed by physicians and industrial feldshers. Their actual proximity to the working place was to facilitate their availability to the workers as well as to minimize the time spent by workers in seeking medical care. How effective those services were is difficult to say, although their massive scope, particularly of preventive measures, appears to have had an impact on reducing work-related mortality and disability. For example, Sigerist notes that during the period of the first five-year plan, the number of accidents at work was reduced by one-half.[41]

Those industrial health centers were administered and operated not by the local Soviets (as the rest of health services were), but by the management of the industrial centers. Their size varied, with some, such as those located in the main steel mills, being large medical and hospital institutions with several hundred beds. Many health centers also maintained day care facilities to assist women workers in the care of their children during working hours. Actually, the creation of such a network of child care centers was aimed primarily at enabling and encouraging women's participation in the labor force. It is important to emphasize that in spite of the dramatic movement of people—particularly the young— from rural to urban areas, there was still a large shortage of manpower, at the same time, incidentally, when the Western world was undergoing the Great Depression with high levels of unemployment everywhere. In the USSR, as in other countries, the great drive for women's liberation was in fact due to the great need for labor.

However, it would be vulgar economic determinism to explain the dramatic advances of women in the USSR as the result only of the pressing need for women's involvement in the labor force and their active participation in the process of production. Without minimizing the importance of those economic factors as enabling factors, they were not the only ones. The Bolshevik Party had a most progressive program for women's liberation, a program that, when implemented after the Ocrtober Revolution, placed the Soviet state far ahead of any country in giving women full civil rights and liberties. Women's rights that are currently being fought for in the United States were accepted and approved by the Soviet Revolution as early as 1917.[42] Still, the actual liberation of women's consciousness developed not only at the legal but also at the economic level, when they became active participants—and very active ones at that— in the process of production. Women were encouraged to work, and they did indeed work in all sectors of industry, including mining, and at the most physically demanding jobs. A delegation of Welsh miners was clearly horrified at seeing women down in the mines doing work they considered too hard for them. Nonetheless, most women worked in those occupations that had traditionally been female, such as medicine and teaching. In that respect, Soviet industrialization meant the further feminization of traditionally female occupations and an initial encroachment on professions still predominantly male. A great enabling factor in that involvement in the labor force was the development of the most massive and extensive network of management-run child care centers ever known in any industrialized country.

The result of women's involvement in the labor force was that the birth rate declined dramatically, particularly in the urban areas. Consequently, and as previously indicated, the ratio within families of working versus nonworking members changed substantially. This dramatic reduction in the birth rate created much concern among the top echelons of the Party, since although advantageous on a short-term basis, a low birthrate would have meant fewer persons in the productive population in the long run. In response to that situation, the 1936 Anti-Abortion Act was passed, which was in fact regressive legislation with respect to the liberation of women. It made abortion on demand, one of the rights won by the October Revolution, illegal, and allowed legal abortion only for therapeutic reasons. Once again, in the USSR as in other countries, women's rights were partially shaped by the needs of the economic system as perceived by those in power in the USSR, i.e., the higher echelons of the Party.

Last but not least, another consequence of the massive industrialization and urbanization of the Soviet Union at that time was the creation of sanitary engineering as an important segment of the health sector. The massive movement of people from rural to urban areas created innumerable problems of crowding, poor housing, and slums. Epidemics, primarily caused by water-borne disease agents, were rampant, creating a great amount of absenteeism. In 1935 the importance of the problem prompted the creation of the State Sanitary Inspectorate under the First Deputy Health Commissar, who was responsible for sanitary work throughout the entire Soviet Union. The primary objective of the Inspectorate was to create a sanitation department responsible for the inspection of the construction of towns and workers' settlements, water and sewage systems, and also industrial hygiene. The State Sanitary Inspectorate mandated that all local Soviets (particularly the urban ones) have a committee responsible for sanitation.

Collectivization of Agriculture and Rural Health Services

The top priority given to industrialization and administering to the problems that were created by urbanization was accompanied by the low priority given to the care of the rural popuation by the central government. Prioritizing industrialization meant, as it generally does, allocating high priority to cities and low priority to rural areas. .This was so, despite the key contribution of the Russian peasantry to "forced saving" and thus to the capitalization required for industrialization. As I indicated earlier, industrialization was based to a large extent on the extraction of surplus from the peasantry. In this process of extraction, however, agricultural production was not centrally administered. Rather, the state farms and cooperatives were given quotas to be fulfilled, to which all their activities were oriented. Within those activities, health services were among the ones considered of low importance. Indeed, health services were the responsibility of the collective farms. And in those farms, "It was the pig-sty and the cow-shed that was important, not the doctor's house. At least one state farm was reported where the last place to be electrified was the hospital."[43] Central governmental intervention was restricted to reminders that health services should be taken care of by the collective farms and local Soviets.

Stalinism in Medicine: Its Industrialization

Contrary to what most writings on health services assume, the health services in the Soviet Union developed not in a centralized, cohesive, and comprehensive fashion (as some central planners would like us to believe), but in an incremental, atomized, and rather disaggregated fashion, with each component of the sector emerging largely in response to specific needs determined by changes in the mode of economic production. Indeed, in the middle 1930s there were preventive stations, industrial preventive and curative centers, environmental sanitation stations, maternal and child care centers, curative clinics, etc., each operated more or less independently of the other and each responsive to different needs and constituencies. Far from being integrated, the health sector of the 1930s was divided into various subsectors and units. In this respect, it is of value to note that strong currents for integration existed, both at the political level among sectors of the Party and at the professional level among the health workers. Proposals had been discussed in the Party as far back as 1929 to create integrated polyclinics, or "unified dispensaries," which would combine under the same roof curative with preventive services, maternal and child care services with adult care services, and sanitary and industrial inspectorates with medical services. These centers would provide comprehensive care to populations living in defined geographical areas. That process of integration of services and their provision to those in need for certain geographically-defined populations had not only a logical but also an equalitarian motivation, i.e., serving everyone living in a certain area, that made it appealing to sectors of the Party as well as to the Commissariat of Health. Contrary to that equalitarian ethos, however, were the needs of industrialization as perceived by the Stalinist leadership of the Party stimulating the inequalities that already existed among occupations and among sectors of the labor force. Indeed, it was Party policy that labor should be rewarded and taken care of in proportion to its productive input into the process of industrialization. And in that respect, the principle of medical service by place of residence was contrary to the preferential service to workers in the leading branches of industry. Thus, the process of integration according to place of residence was repudiated. Instead, services were grouped according to the main functional areas needed for the process of industrialization, including (a) industrial and sanitary medicine (incorporating preventive medicine), (b) maternal and child care, and (c) curative medicine given in polyclinics. At that time, the hospital was to provide supportive services to these polyclinics.

*The Effect of Industrialization on the Specialization of
Medicine: A Further Division of Labor*

Until 1929, which was the initial year of planned industrialization, medical education was similar to the pattern prevalent in most continental European countries. It was much influenced by the German school, whose medical curriculum reflected a mechanistic approach towards medicine. Indeed, the medical world at that time in Europe (and, via the Flexner Report and the influence of Johns Hopkins, in North America as well) was greatly influenced by industrialization and technology, the prevalent ideological constructs of the developist bourgeoisie. Disease was supposed to be caused by a dysfunction of a machine, the body of the individual. That mechanistic concept of medicine was incorporated into most medical curriculums of Europe, including prerevolutionary Russia. Still, when the October Revolution occurred, medical education remained largely unaltered. The changes that did occur were more quantitative than qualitative. One change expanded the number of years required for obtaining an adequate medical education from three to four years, with the addition of preventive medicine and hygiene (primarily occupational hygiene) as disciplines. The changes that occurred were primarily concerned with the questions of for whom services should be provided and who would provide them, rather than with the redefinition of medicine and its curriculum. The number of medical schools increased dramatically, as did the number of students. Moreover, the majority of the new students possessed different class backgrounds, i.e., working class and peasantry, than had been traditionally the case. However, medicine, the meaning of medicine, and its instruction remained basically the same. In U.S. terms, Soviet medicine continued to be very "Flexnerian" in approach.

The industrialization of Soviet society and the ethos of productivity and specialization led to a further strengthening of that vision of medicine, with the division of medical studies in 1938 into three main branches: general medicine (therapy and industrial preventive medicine), maternity and child care (later to become pediatrics), and sanitation and hygiene (to become public health). This specialization of medical studies from the beginning of the student's educational program was largely the result of (1) the need expressed by the Party to divide health services into these three main areas to meet the demands of industrialization, as described in the previous section, and (2) the basic mechanistic conception of medicine, separating medicine in terms of function and population group to be served. That division formally established and perpetuated the division between environmental and individual medicine, and between preventive and curative medicine—main cleavages characteristic of Flexnerian medical education. And although the Soviet system gave far more importance to preventive medicine and services than did Western medicine, the conception of medicine remained split into categories that were imported from the Western world. In that respect, the division of labor in the health sector, which in a socialist society should have declined, instead increased.

*The Effect of Industrialization on the Composition of the
Labor Force in the Health Sector: Its Feminization and
Hierarchicalization of the Health Labor Force*

The process of industrialization also had a profound effect on the sex and occupational composition of the labor force. The productive sectors of the economy, referred to in political economy as the primary sectors, were given far higher priority than the supportive or service sectors. Skills, trades, and tools involved in production were more highly valued and rewarded than those necessary in services. Consequently, an engineer had more prestige and received higher rewards than did a service worker, such as a physician. In a situation of manpower shortage, women, as the last to join the labor force, although participating in practically all sectors of the labor force, predominated in those sectors that enjoyed less prestige, e.g., health services. Thus, the majority of health workers were women. Also, health work was considered at that time to be more in line with the feminine mystique. In the middle of this period (1934), women represented 92 percent of all workers in the health sector and 75 percent of all physicians. Here it is important to answer a point that is frequently raised in U.S. feminist circles, specifically that the large percentage of women in medicine in the Soviet Union explains the apparently low prestige of the medical profession in that country. In fact, however, historical events show that precisely the reverse is true. The lower prestige of service occupations was due not to the predominance of women but to the heavy emphasis on industrialization and the higher priority given to the productive sectors of the economy. Therefore, it was not the increased feminization of medicine during that process that caused its relatively lower prestige but rather the reverse. To put it bluntly, the second-rate workers—women—were to perform the second-rate jobs.

While much has been said about the feminization of medicine, little has been discussed about the class-ization and hierarchicalization of medicine that also developed during this period. As shown and previously discussed, the immediate effect of the Soviet Revolution had been to make university education available to members of the working class and their children. In that respect, the changes in the class extraction of medical students were quite dramatic immediately after the October Revolution.

The emphasis on specialization and expertise that accompanied the process of industrialization, however, and the concomitant effect already described on the restoration of hierarchies of labor were also replicated in the health sector. A process of specialization in medicine appeared, in which the hospital-based specialist and specialty were more important than the generalist, and both specialist and generalist were more important and better paid than the other personnel, such as nurses and feldshers.

Moreover, the establishment of criteria for acceptance to higher university education, including medicine, which were dependent on prior scholastic performance regardless of social class or place of origin of the applicant, had a dramatic effect in changing the class composition of the medical student body, with the majority of students coming from white-collar and not from blue-collar families. In that respect, the establishment of criteria of performance, when the definition of performance had not changed, determined a strengthening of class controls over the composition of the student body.

The Effect of Industrialization in the Structure of the Health Sector: Its Centralization and Hospital Orientation

The need for the Party to direct the process of industrialization required further expansion and centralization of the bureaucracy responsible for either guiding or actually administering the different sectors of the economy, including the health services. This need for centralization demanded the creation, in 1936, of a double accountability in the health sector that continued until the late 1950s. In 1936 the basic organizational structure of Soviet health services was established, creating the Ministry of Public Health as the supreme administrative authority in the health sector. The Minister, always a physician, was and is a member of the Cabinet. The Cabinet and entire government reported and still report to the Executive Committee of the Party.

Below the Ministry were the Republic Ministries of Health, and under them the *oblast* and *rayon* health departments, in that order. At each level the chief administrator was appointed by his superior, and was accountable to him in terms of policy and administration. On the other hand, the chief administrator was also a member of the Soviet administration, and as such, administratively accountable to the Soviet authorities, whether at the republic, rayon, or oblast level. In practice as well as in theory, however, the primary responsibility was to the central and vertical line of command, emanating initially from the Party through the USSR Ministry. The Ministry in Moscow had the final responsibility in decision making. A well-defined hierarchy was established, replicating the bureaucratic hierarchicalization that appeared in most organs of the state in the USSR during that time. For example, during that period, no fewer than thirty grades were established in the Civil Services, each one having an insignia and specific service ranks. That hierarchicalization touched on every aspect of life, widening the system of rewards and increasing the wage differentials between and within occupations. At the top were the chief echelons of the Party and the technocracy. In the health sector, the specialized medical experts—the medical academicians—comprised the chief health technocracy that was responsible for establishing norms and standards for that sector. Below this normative level there was the administrative structure, in which all administrative heads of ministries, health departments, and institutions had to be physicians, with the top director usually a surgeon, and the assistant director a public health physician and/or epidemiologist.

Let me add that this hierarchicalization and specialization also had implications for the internal priorities within the health system. Within the organization of health services, the hospital was increasingly considered as the central axis for the entire system. Indeed, a very massive hospital construction program started at that time. And many reasons have been given for that massive hospital orientation of medicine that has led the Soviet Union to be the country with the highest bed-per-capita ratio in the world. The most frequent reason given by the Soviet health authorities was the poor housing conditions of the time, which made the care of patients at home unsafe and unmedical. I would postulate that, however important the housing situation may have been to the need for hospitals that could take care of the inpatient needs of the population, there are other variables far more important to explain it, i.e., (1) the increased specialization in medicine, and (2) the specialized nature of academic medicine, with control by academic medicine of the normative function of the Ministry. For academic medicine, good medicine was hospital medicine. Actually, this increased reliance on the hospital was formalized in the Polyclinic Hospital Reorganization Act of 1947, where it was believed that in order to raise the standards of medical care and improve doctors' qualifications, the polyclinics should be amalgamated with the hospitals. It is interesting to mention the reasons given for that integration, since they are also largely present in today's debate on the reorganization of health services, both in Great Britain as well as in the United States. Those reasons were (1) that doctors were working in isolation from the hospital and the centralized technology placed there, and (2) that a lack of continuity of care existed when the patient was hospitalized. This discontinuity was due to the division of responsibilities, with the care of the hospitalized patient assigned to a physician different from the ambulatory care physician. The consequence of that lack of continuity, in addition to a lack of coordination between hospitals and polyclinics, was an increase in the unnecessary use of hospital services.

As a result of that integration, hospital specialists were to work in the polyclinic, while the therapist (the ambulatory care doctor) was to work in the hospital for four months every one and one-half years.[44]

The result of this act was that the health center was absorbed by the hospital.

As Hyde emphasizes, the reform led to a setback for the polyclinic and its absorption by the hospital.[45] And it also affected unfavorably the preventive services that were provided in ambulatory centers. In theory, according to the Act those services were to be provided by the hospital, but in practice, hospitals failed to deliver them. The integration of services under the auspices of the hospital also meant the predominance of the hospital over all other services, including ambulatory and preventive services.

Actually, this integration of all branches under the hospital went even further in 1956 with the reorganization of health services administration, in which the sanitary-epidemiological station was also integrated with the hospital, with the hospital being responsible for the delivery of those services. According to this reorganization, the chief of the rayon hospital was to be both the head of the rayon health department and the one responsible for the provision of the sanitary-epidemiological services. The battle for integration was won by academic and hospital-based medicine, which controlled the normative function of the Central Ministry, and integrated the separate parts of the health sector under the direction of the hospital.

5

Post-Stalinism: Khrushchev
and After

By the time of Stalin's death in March of 1953, the generation of the Soviet people who were in their sixties had experienced three major wars and much hardship, particularly in the campaign for massive industrialization which had emphasized production and deemphasized consumption. As the preamble to the new Social Security Act of 1956 indicated: "Our generation has experienced three major wars, has borne on its shoulders all the hardships of the reconstruction of the national economy, and for this it has used much of its strength and health."[1] That generation and also the younger ones had been responsible for the most dramatic and massive transformation of their country from a backward society to the second-largest industrial power in the world. And that transformation had been achieved at great sacrifice and cost. Khrushchev and the new leadership represented an intent of relaxation and limited liberalization in the task that still lay ahead. Indeed, the death of Stalin triggered a series of events that led to the establishment of a new leadership in the Communist Party, which initiated what is usually referred to as the process of "de-Stalinization." Let us analyze the different components of that process at the political, economic, and social levels.

At the political level, the most important event occurred at the Twentieth Congress of the Communist Party in 1956 in which Nikita Khrushchev delivered his famous "secret" speech, wherein he denounced Stalin in the strongest terms ever used by any political figure up to that time. In his criticism, Khrushchev stated that Stalin had hindered rather than advanced the process of Soviet industrialization, and showed how the Stalinist repression of large sectors of the Party, the citizenry, and the army had erected serious obstacles against victory over the Nazis and the process of Soviet reconstruction altogether. Also, he accused Stalin's leadership of being arbitrary and responsible for perpetrating monstrous crimes against the Soviet people. The intention of Khrushchev's speech was to disassociate the new leadership of the Party from the large number of hardships imposed on the Soviet citizens which the new leadership felt had been unnecessary and arbitrary.

Other changes initiated by the new leadership of the Party were, at the economic level, the decentralization of the state apparatus and the attention given to the consumer and agricultural sectors and, at the social level, the revamping and restructuring of the social security system. Due to the importance of those changes for the present composition and distribution of the social sectors, let us analyze them in further detail.

Decentralization of the State Apparatus as a Strategy for Central Control

A major change during the Khrushchev era was the decentralization of the central governmental agencies, with the establishment of regional bodies (*sovnark-hozy*) responsible for the implementation of economic and social policies. Among the responsibilities of those regional bodies were the appointments of the directors and managers of the economic enterprises, who were given far more autonomy than they had during the previous period (1938-1952). Later on, in 1965, managerial autonomy was further expanded to include the managers' power to define the work rhythm, the overall size of employment in the firm, and the internal distribution of wages. These reforms have led many authors to the conclusion that the planning machinery in the Soviet Union had been dismantled and that market forces were reinstated as the mechanism for regulating the final allocation of resources.[2] It is highly inaccurate, however, to assume that the decentralization of the central governmental agencies and the limited autonomy of economic enterprises did in fact amount to a dismantling of the planning machinery and the reinstatement of market forces.

Actually, the regional bodies were part of the state apparatus, and their responsibility was one of implementing the state plans. As Carlo indicates, a primary motivation for decentralization of the central agencies was to increase rather than diminish the power of the central political bodies by (1) expanding the state apparatus and moving it closer to the point of actual implementation, and (2) adding more flexibility to that implementation, bypassing the central agencies or ministries considered to be too rigid for the smooth implementation of the plans.[3] But even that experience with decentralization was short-lived. In 1965, the regional bodies were dismissed and their power was integrated with the newly strengthened central administrating agencies. As to the autonomy of enterprises, it was only relative. Indeed, the most important decisions in each enterprise, i.e., goods to be produced, capital investments in new plants to be built, production to be sold, unit prices, total wage fund, levels of profit and of income, and many other key decisions were and still are controlled by state regulations, were and still must be approved by state departments, and did and still must fall within the overall plans.[4]

The economy, then, is planned by the central state agencies, following the policy directions of the top echelons of the Party. Needless to say, there are strong pressures, such as the one led by the Liberman school,[5] to establish the market as the proper mechanism to determine the level of prices, wages, and the allocation of resources, which may, at the end, influence and be accepted by the present leadership. In this respect, it is of interest to single out the great support that this leadership gave to Viklow's experiments, in which sectors of the textile industry were managed autonomously and exclusively according to the principle of profitability.[6]

The Agricultural Policies: Resurrection from Oblivion

The priorities given to massive industrialization, and the relative neglect of the agricultural sectors, had determined a large movement of people from the rural to the urban areas which created problems of labor surplus in the urban areas and scarcity in the rural ones—a scarcity that was particularly marked among the productive age groups of the Russian population. Actually, in many regions during the 1960s, the average age of the agricultural population approached fifty years. That situation undoubtedly worried the leadership of that time, and still worries today's leadership. Thus a series of measures were implemented by the Soviet authorities to make agricultural work and its pay more attractive, including the expansion of social security (until 1964 limited to workers of state farms) to all agricultural workers. Also, the salary of agricultural workers was increased, an increase which was aimed at diminishing the wage differentials between industrial and agricultural workers. Last, but certainly not least, the priority given to agricultural production was reflected in the 1962 division of the Communist Party into two branches, the industrial and the agricultural branches. And as Meissner indicates, that policy was aimed not only at better directing and controlling agricultural production, but also at enhancing the social status of the kolkhoz peasants and agricultural workers.[7]

Labor Policies and Social Security

The increased attention and emphasis given by the new leadership of the Party to the consumer and light industry sectors of the economy required structural changes in the patterns of economic production which demanded substantial changes in some of the labor policies operating at the time of de-Stalinization. One of the required changes was the need for labor mobility, both from enterprise to enterprise and also from one economic sector to another. Thus, the labor law which was established during the period of industrialization and which required workers to work for the enterprise to which they were assigned, was discontinued in 1956 to allow for labor mobility.[8]

Moreover, labor and social legislation was implemented to favor retraining and upward mobility.[9] Reflecting these policies were (1) the reopening of the evening medical colleges in which adult workers (mostly paraprofessionals) could undertake medical studies leading to a medical degree, and (2) the reestablishing of social class origin of the applicant as an important criterion for acceptance in the institutions of higher learning, including medical schools. This last policy, however, seems to have been largely ignored or only infrequently implemented.

But the most profound labor policy changes were in the social security programs, particularly in the extension of benefits, broadening of population coverage, and amount of resources available for the programs. Regarding the expansion of benefits, the most important change was the new Pension Plan of 1958 that corrected large inadequacies in the previous plans. Indeed, by 1958, the maximum pension was below the officially-defined subsistence level.[10] In the new plan, benefits were greatly increased, doubling the rate that was considered minimal, with the rate structure changed to favor not the ones with higher incomes at the time of their retirement, as in Stalin's time, but those in the lower income brackets. Also, the age of retirement was lowered to sixty years (from sixty-five years) for men, and to fifty-five years (from sixty years) for women. That retirement age was considerably lower for occupations involving hard or unhealthy work, underground and hot environments, and disabled individuals.[11] The reasons for the implementation of the new Pension Plan were many, but prominent among them were the demographic changes that were taking place, with an absolute as well as a relative increase in the elderly sector of the population. By 1959, there were 19.1 million people over sixty years of age, 11.5 million of them no longer working. As the act establishing the pension plan had indicated, they had done quite enough for the system, and it was time that the elderly received some benefits in return. Needless to say, the new Pension Plan of 1958 was also an important strategy for legitimizing the new leadership of the Party. It showed that "they cared." And the people's demand for care was made increasingly loud and clear.[12]

Complementing that popular pension plan was the Disability Plan of 1963, which also increased the level of benefits and equalized them. By this I mean that the benefits received by a worker depended less on the sector of the economy to which he or she belonged, as in Stalin's time, and more on the years of work and nature of the disability. As to the expansion of the population coverage, the most important change was the act of 1969, when social security benefits were expanded to cover all agricultural workers as well. And last, but certainly not least, there was a relative and absolute increase in the amount of overall resources available for the social security programs. Their percentage of state budget expenditures rose from 4.4 percent in 1950 to 10.2 percent in 1965. According to International Labor Organization computations, this latter percentage compared favorably with that of the United States (6.2 percent), but unfavorably with France (14.6 percent), Sweden (13.5 percent), Italy (12.8 percent), and the U.K. (11.2).[13]

Final Comments: Elements of Continuity Between Stalin's Period and After

An increasing debate among Sovietologists has developed around the question as to whether there was a profound change in the Soviet system after Stalin. Actually, a large sector believes that there was indeed a qualitative as well as a quantitative change from socialism (assumed to exist during Stalin's time) to capitalism (assumed to exist today).

An analysis of productive and social policies, however, indicates that while substantial changes have taken place since the time of Stalin's death, these changes have primarily included (1) a slight increase in the consumer sectors, (2) a large increase in the social security sectors, and (3) a change in the administrative direction of the state apparatus toward giving a limited amount of autonomy to the economic units of production. But both the direction and nature of the productive and social sectors (as we have seen with social security in this section, and as we will see with the health sector in the next one) have not changed.

Actually, an analysis of the economic and social policies and structures of the present USSR (as I will present in the following sections) shows these to be based on policies and structures developed, for the most part, during Stalin's period. For example, the policy of declaring the CPSU "the party of the people and not only of the working class" and the concomitant change in the social class background of the Party's membership (from blue collar to white collar) were not, as Martin Nicolaus reports,[14] declared and implemented by Khrushchev, but rather, as I indicated before, by Stalin.

Indeed, as Miliband points out, to suggest that a qualitative change took place in the Soviet system after Stalin's death is to assume a cult of personality in reverse, i.e., to assume that in the period 1928-1953 all good (as the neo-Stalinists postulate) or all bad (as Khrushchev and the present Soviet leadership seem to indicate) was due to one person, Stalin. Paradoxically, this un-Marxian position seems to be held by some sectors of the present Chinese leadership as well.

But this personalistic vision (in which history is perceived as a succession of historical figures) is misleading and inaccurate. Indeed, history is both the combination of objective (material) and subjective (including ideologies and personalities) conditions. Stalinism was not just due to Stalin. And although he gave a personal imprimatur—and a very important one at that—to the Soviet system during the period that he held power, the system would not have been entirely different without him. As Miliband says:

This is *not* to argue that Stalinism was the work and the responsibility of one man; that too is untenable. But it is nevertheless entirely reasonable, indeed inescapably necessary, to see Stalin as having played a crucial role in the particular character which the Soviet system assumed during the years of his rule: in other words, the system would have functioned very differently without him—even though it would not have been an entirely different system.[15]

In summary, and as Sweezy and Bettelheim[16] have indicated, the reasons for what are considered to be the present characteristics of the Soviet system are not to be found in the question of the personalities of the present leaders, but rather in the objective and subjective forces, briefly defined in the course of the previous sections, which determined the specific nature of the present Soviet economic and social systems.

6

The Present Structure of the
Soviet Health Sector[a]

Levels of Care

From the previous sections dealing with the evolution of the health sector in different periods, we can see that the present Soviet health care sector is an aggregate of distinct elements that historically appeared at different moments in time in response to the specific needs of the mode of production of the Soviet economy, needs as perceived by the main controllers of that society's political power. The basic structure of the Soviet medical care system at present is briefly presented in Figure 6-1.

At the *primary care level*, we find the uchastock hospitals, or polyclinics, which provide the primary and ambulatory secondary and tertiary health care services for a population of approximately 40,000 inhabitants; the residents of the political unit called uchastock. The primary care services are specialized and grouped according to the three main categories previously discussed, i.e., general or adult medicine, pediatrics, and public health. Primary care services are primarily provided by the uchastock therapist (internist) who is responsible for 2,000 to 2,500 adults in the prescribed area. The uchastock pediatrician is responsible for 750 to 1,250 children up to the age of fifteen years living in the area, and, in some instances, there is an uchastock occupational physician for every 1,000 to 2,000 workers of large industrial units located in the area of the polyclinics who, besides providing medical care for the workers assigned to him, also inspects and supervises the conditions of work.[1] These physicians usually have complete access to pathological, electrocardiographic, and X-ray examinations, as well as to an extensive cadre of secondary and tertiary care specialists who work in the polyclinic on a full-time basis. In the rural areas, a system of allied-health stations has been established with the feldsher stations being the most important. They are responsible for providing (1) first contact care, (2) prenatal and postnatal care, and (3) the supervision of infants. These stations are functionally and administratively independent of the uchastock polyclinics.

A perfunctory analysis of the structure of primary care indicates the following characteristics:

First, primary care is divided into the three main areas of medicine: general

---

[a]Most of the information presented in this chapter was gathered in the course of my visits to the Central Ministry of Health of the USSR and to the Semaschko Institute.

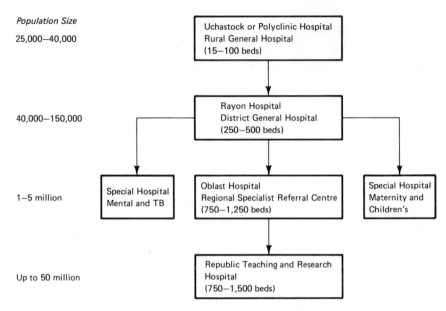

Source: Adapted from J. Fry, *Medicine in Three Societies* (New York: American Elsevier, 1970), p. 122.

Figure 6-1. Structure of the Medical Care System in the USSR

or adult care, maternal and child care, and preventive and environmental (including occupational) medicine. Each of these branches operates functionally as well as administratively independent of the other, and (in urban areas) the care provided can be sited in different types of polyclinics altogether.[2] There is no coordinating individual, unit, or team that can relate the care provided by the pediatrician to the child with the care provided by the therapist to the adults of the same family. As Fry reports: "There is no sign or trend of any family teams providing cooperative care for the family group as a whole and it is not considered necessary to reintroduce any family physician."[3] The aforementioned industrialization of medicine and subsequent specialization are carried to the primary care level as well.

Second, there is a clear separation of responsibilities between primary, and secondary and tertiary care specialists. The former (primary care) is a referral point within the system, sending patients to the latter when required. Actually, Ryan reports unhappiness among some of the primary care physicians who are resentful of being considered "mere qualified dispatchers" by the secondary and tertiary care specialists.[4] Moreover, not unlike other countries where Flexnerian medicine is hegemonic, a hierarchy seems to have been established in which primary care physicians are less esteemed than secondary and tertiary care ones.

Third, there is a clear distinction between ambulatory and hospital care. Physicians working in the polyclinic for the most part do not work in the hospital, nor do physicians working in the hospital work in the polyclinic. In theory, primary care physicians are allowed (since 1965) to work in the hospital three to four months every one and a half to two years.[5] But, according to Ryan, this situation seems to be more theoretical than actual. It is interesting to note here that this separation between ambulatory and hospital care was primarily a response to the absorption of the polyclinic by the hospital as a result of the previously defined Hospital Act of 1947. At that time, the polyclinic physicians were supposed to work two hours a day in the hospital. But in that polyclinic-hospital relationship, "the polyclinic came off badly."[6] Most of the resources were absorbed by the hospital, with the health center perceived as an appendix to the hospital. And the discontinuation of that working arrangement, whereby physicians working in polyclinics were allowed and even encouraged to work in the hospital, was due to the planners' perceived need of slowing down that integration and the absorption of the polyclinic by the hospital.

Secondary inpatient care is provided in the district or rayon hospitals, with 200 to 500 hospital beds, which take care of inpatient services for the population of the district or rayon which ranges in size from 40,000 to 150,000 people. The rayon hospitals are staffed with full-time specialists working exclusively in inpatient care. Super-specialized or *tertiary inpatient care* is provided in the oblast hospitals, which usually have 800 to 1,200 beds and are responsible for the provision of services to a population living in an oblast or region of approximately 1 to 5 million people. Also at this level are special maternal and childrens' hospitals, as well as hospitals for mental and infectious diseases. All physicians employed in these hospitals work full time in inpatient care. Apart from these three levels, there are the republic and nationwide institutions that provide specialized care for specific research purposes, e.g., the National Cancer Research Institute in Moscow.

It is interesting to note the full-time commitment to inpatient care of all physicians working in hospitals. The consequences of this arrangement are many, but some deserve special attention. First, there is a lack of continuity of care, with the care provided to the individual being the responsibility of different physicians, depending on whether the patient is in a horizontal (hospital) or vertical (ambulatory) position. Second, there is a lack of coordination between hospital and ambulatory care, a lack of coordination that, incidentally, leads on occasion to unnecessary hospitalization. For example, in a research project carried out in the town of Uryupwisk, it was found that 28 percent of inpatients could have been treated in domiciliary care under the supervision of a primary care physician.[7]

The Administrative Structure of the Soviet Health Services

The administrative structure of the Soviet health sector is depicted in Figure 6-2. At the top is the Ministry of Health of the USSR, the main policy and

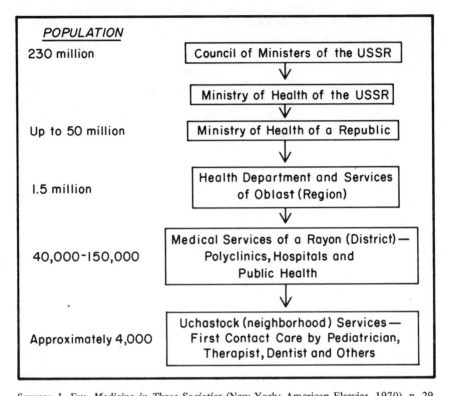

POPULATION

230 million	Council of Ministers of the USSR
	Ministry of Health of the USSR
Up to 50 million	Ministry of Health of a Republic
1.5 million	Health Department and Services of Oblast (Region)
40,000-150,000	Medical Services of a Rayon (District) — Polyclinics, Hospitals and Public Health
Approximately 4,000	Uchastock (neighborhood) Services — First Contact Care by Pediatrician, Therapist, Dentist and Others

Source: J. Fry, *Medicine in Three Societies* (New York: American Elsevier, 1970), p. 29.

Figure 6-2. Structure of the Administration of the Health Care Sector in the USSR

planning body, led by the Minister, currently a well-known cardiosurgeon, who combines clinical with administrative responsibilities. The Ministry is responsible for (1) the implementation of the National Health Policies as defined by the Executive Committee of the Party and approved by the Cabinet (of which the Minister is a member); (2) the planning functions, with the approval and establishment of the norms and standards of care prepared by the prestigious Institute of the National Academy of Sciences, the Semaschko Institute, which is, as will be discussed later, heavily dominated by academic medicine; and (3) the preparation and implementation of the National Health Budget, within the overall five-year plan, and prospective budgets prepared by the main planning body, the Gozplan or Central Planning Council.

The staff of the Ministry is made up of only 900 full-time civil servants, of which the majority are physicians who work there at the pinnacle of their professional careers in the branch of administrative medicine. Compared with health ministries in other countries, the size of the staff is relatively small. Indeed, in the United States the health side of the Department of Health, Education and Welfare employs 12,000 professionals. The smallness of the staff in the USSR is due to the fact that its function is one primarily of policy-making and not of administration, and also that the responsibility for functions such as the administration of research and training is delegated to other centers, e.g., the Academy of Medical Sciences of the USSR, of which the Semaschko Institute (responsible for the preparation of norms and standards) is part.

Each one of the fifteen republics has its own Ministry of Health, headed by a Minister. That Minister is appointed by the Federal Minister of Health, subject to approval by the Soviet Council of Ministers (Cabinet) of the Republic. The main policies as well as budget priorities come from above, from the National Ministry, and must be approved by the republic Cabinet. Most of the republican budget is derived from central governmental funds and is not based on republican, regional, or local taxation. Needless to say, this situation gives almost total control, both in policy-making and budgeting, to the central government.

While policy making and budgeting are carried out primarily at the national and, less importantly, republic levels, the detailed administration is done at the regional or oblast level. The size of a region or oblast is approximately 1 to 5 million people, with large cities such as Leningrad (4.5 million people) functioning as oblasts. The region has an Executive Committee of the regional Soviet elected by the oblast population. The Chief Medical Officer is a member of that committee, and has full-time administrative responsibility for all the health services and institutions of the region. He is also the director of the regional or oblast hospital, and is responsible for the administration of (1) all clinical services given in the districts and polyclinics within the region; (2) all public health services given in the districts and polyclinics; and (3) all industrial and preventive services given in the polyclinics. It is worth mentioning here that the actual responsibility for the medical direction of the clinical services is allocated to the chiefs of the clinical departments of the main regional hospital. For example, the director of surgery at the regional hospital is responsible for and in charge of all surgical services and units provided at the regional, district, and polyclinic levels. He is also responsible for insuring adequate postgraduate training for that specialty.

The regions are divided into administrative units or districts whose boundaries are identical to the political boundaries of the rayon (population ranging in number from 40,000 to 150,000 inhabitants). All district health facilities are under the administrative responsibility of the chief physician of the district, who is appointed by the oblast Chief Medical Officer. As a rule the chief physician is also the director of the district hospital and bears the administrative responsibility for the services provided by the district hospital as well as by the polyclinics. It is important to note that the clinicians working in either the district hospital or polyclinics have a dual responsibility in that they are clinically responsible to the regional chief of their specialty, and administratively responsible to the head of their center.

The Political Determinants of the Structure in the Soviet
Health Sector

As a result of the previously-described historical events, we find that a pattern of health services and a system of administration have been established in the USSR that contain the following well-defined characteristics: (1) a centralized system of planning and administration; (2) a highly specialized structure; and (3) a regionalized system of care. Let me focus on the last two characteristics, both of which, as I will try to show, are much the result of the control exercised by specific groups over the centralized system of planning and administration. Indeed, as we have seen, the system of regionalization in the USSR is highly specialized, with health services divided into three main categories: adult medicine, pediatric care, and public health and industrial medicine. These categories are functionally as well as administratively separate from each other. Moreover, besides these vertical categories, we also find horizontal categories within a hierarchical order: tertiary care inpatient, secondary care inpatient, tertiary and secondary care outpatient, and primary care outpatient. The separation among those levels is clear-cut, with the patient being treated by different personnel depending on which one of these categories he fits into.

Within these different functional groupings, there is a well-defined flow of both providers of care and patients, in which care at each level is performed after referral from a previous level. Figure 6–3 depicts this functional division of care in the Soviet health system. Within that pattern of referrals, there is a pattern of hierarchies, the tertiary inpatient specialist being at the top and the primary care generalist at the bottom. In our historical review, I have explained the moments at which those hierarchies appeared and also given my own theory of why they appeared. Indeed, the reader may recall that the basic infrastructure for the administration of the health system was established in two periods: one in 1937, in the basic restructuring of the entire Soviet administration by Stalin; and the other more recently in 1965, with the integration of all health services under the axis of the hospital sector.

In summary, that structure reflects and translates the patterns of political and technical dominance over the past and present administrative structure of the Soviet health sector. Within the hierarchical order established in the Soviet health sector, we find at the very top, the leaders of the Party who are committed to capital accumulation via massive industrialization. This is a commitment which also implies a delegation of their authority to the "experts," i.e., the ones who know, in theory, how to run the specific economic or social activities of the system. In the health sector, the members of the medical profession are considered to be the experts.

Within that profession, we have at the very top, members of academic medicine, who exert a dominant influence over the normative functions of the planning machinery. They also control the information that reaches the decision makers or top Party echelons. And that pattern of dominance explains why the advice that

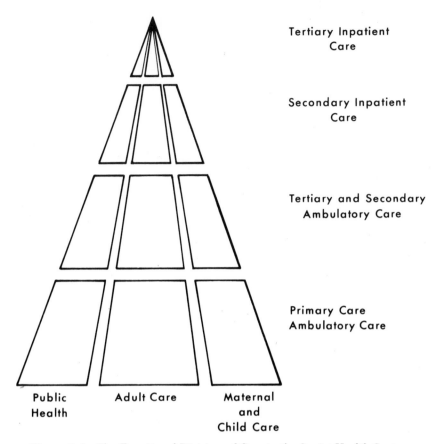

Tertiary Inpatient
Care

Secondary Inpatient
Care

Tertiary and Secondary
Ambulatory Care

Primary Care
Ambulatory Care

Public   Adult Care   Maternal
Health   and
                                 Child Care

Figure 6-3. The Functional Division of Care in the Soviet Health System

reaches the top of the centralized political structure is highly biased toward specialized, hospital-based medicine. Needless to say, this bias further strengthens
the ideological construct of the political system, i.e., specialized management
of society.

Once the plans are accepted, their implementation is also highly centralized,
with the authority coming from the top to the bottom (see Chapter 9 for a description of the Soviet planning machinery). And within that machinery, academic and
specialized medicine have very important roles. Indeed, as I have indicated, (1) the
director of the regional hospital is the director of the entire regional health system,
and (2) the chiefs of the clinical departments are the heads of all the services for
that region. Academic and specialized medicine do establish, then, (1) a predominance of the hospital over all other components of the health sector, and (2) a
highly specialized structure for the whole health sector.

7

The Health Labor Force in the Soviet Union

The Growth and Composition of the Health Labor Force

The changes in the mode of production of the Soviet economy during the last three decades have altered the size and composition of the Soviet labor force, with a rapid growth in the manual sector of the labor force, a slower growth in the white-collar sector, and a steady decline in the agricultural sector, as shown in Table 7-1.

As one would expect, and as shown in Table 7-2, the majority of manual workers are employed in the primary and secondary sectors of the economy (industry, transportation, communication, and trade) while the white-collar workers are employed in the tertiary sectors (social services, and state and social administration). It is interesting to note, incidentally, the different sex composition within each sector of the economy. Women represent almost 40 percent of the labor force in manufacturing, transportation, and communications; 52 percent of all agricultural workers (65 percent of all individual peasants in the private sector); and 71 percent of the labor force in the tertiary sectors.[1]

In the evolution of the labor force, there has been (1) an increased concentration of that force in the urban areas, and (2) an increased income differentiation among varying occupational levels within and among the different sectors of the labor force. T.B. Bottomore has estimated, for example, that the ratio between the income of a factory manager to that of a manual worker is 25 to 1.[2]

As part of these changes in the overall labor force, the health sector has also grown considerably during the subsequent period of industrialization, although less than the manufacturing sectors. For example, while the growth in the number of physicians has indeed been quite dramatic—from 63,200 in 1928 to 460,000 in 1963—still, the number of engineers grew from 47,000 to 1,420,000 during the same period.[3] Table 7-3 shows the growth in the main categories of personnel in the health sector from 1940 to 1972.

All told, there were in 1964, for a population of 226,253,000 people, 3,933,000 persons employed in all branches of the health services, or approximately 1.77 percent of the total population and 5.6 percent of the wage and salary earners (70,526,000) in the Soviet Union.[4] Altogether, 12.8 percent were professionals, 39 percent paraprofessionals, and 48 percent members of the health services category, including cooks, drivers, launderers, janitorial, and other personnel. Table 7-4 presents the numerical distribution of physicians and paraprofessional health personnel in the Soviet health labor force for 1972.

Table 7-1

Estimated Percentages of the Occupational Structure of the Soviet Labor Force 1940–1970[a]

	1940 %	1950 %	1960 %	1970 %
Primary and Secondary Sectors of the Economy				
Industry, transportation, communication, and trade:				
Blue-collar workers	20	25	33	48
White-collar workers	9	10	10.5	12
Agricultural workers	45	44	35	—
Peasants	9.5	2	0.3	—
Others	4	—[b]	—	—
Tertiary Sectors of the Economy				
White-Collar and service workers in education and health	6	7.7	10	12
Housing, welfare, public transportation, administration of state, social organizations, and credit and insurance	6.2	6.1	5.7	5.2
Total (1970)				
120 million				

Sources: Adapted from Boris Meissner, *Social Change in the Soviet Union* (Indiana: University of Notre Dame Press, 1972), Tables 4 and 10; David Lane, *Politics and Society in the USSR* (New York: Random House, 1970), Chapter 12; and W.W. Eason, "Population Changes," in Cyril E. Black (ed.), *The Transformation of Russian Society* (Cambridge: Harvard University Press, 1960), Table 5.

[a]Statistical information on Soviet occupational structure follows different criteria than U.S. data. The U.S. category white-collar workers tends to correspond, however, to the Soviet category non-manual office workers.

[b]No data.

The Growth and Composition of Medical Personnel

The production of physicians has been most dramatic, growing twenty-onefold since the October Revolution, while the population of the country increased by only one third, making the USSR the country with the second-highest density of physicians (after Israel), with all physicians being trained in their own country. Table 7-5 compares the growth in the number of physicians registered in the USSR with those in the United States. It is interesting to note that in the growth of the number of physicians, the largest increases took place when facilities such as the previously discussed evening medical colleges were created, enabling the

Table 7–2

Estimated Employment in Various Sectors of the Soviet Economy, 1960

Economic Sectors	Blue-Collar Workers %	White-Collar Workers %	Agricultural Workers %
Manufacturing, communications, transportation and trade	65	30	1.3
Social services, and state and social administration	11	46	0.3
Other	24	24	98.4
Total	100	100	100

Source: Adapted from Boris Meissner, *Social Change in the Soviet Union* (Indiana: University of Notre Dame Press, 1972), p. 82.

Table 7–3

Physicians and Paramedical Personnel in the Soviet Health Labor Force (in thousands)

	1940	1960	1965	1970	1972
Medical (including dentists)	155.3	413	554	668	731
Paramedical personnel[a]	472	1388	1691	2123	2269

Source: *Manpower Statistics, 1940–1972* (Moscow: Central Statistical Office, 1975). (In Russian)

[a]Includes feldshers, midwives, medical laboratory technicians, X-ray technicians, and dental assistants.

adult working population to obtain an university education. Examples of these increases were those that occurred in the early university reform during Lenin's time and the second reform during Khrushchev's time, particularly in the period 1960–1963. These later reforms were aimed primarily at augmenting the in-service education of paramedical and other types of workers.

Let me now analyze not only the size but also the composition of the medical profession. And here again we find that in order to explain the Soviet production of medical personnel, we have to go outside the health sector. Indeed, in discussing the genesis, nature, and expression of Stalinism, I underlined that Stalinism was characterized by the control of production by a political body (the *CPSU*) whose aim was to optimize the process of capital accumulation via the process of industrialization, industrialization as understood by both Western and Eastern camps at that time. It was also at that time, as I indicated, that Soviet medicine was basically established in the early reforms of 1932, reforms

Table 7-4
Professional and Paraprofessional Health Personnel, USSR, 1972
(excluding the military)

Physicians by Specialization		
Therapists[a]	153,400	
Surgeons[b]	76,900	
Obstetricians-gynecologists	45,900	
Pediatricians	88,800	
Ophthalmologists	17,000	
Otorhinolaryngologists	17,200	
Neuropathologists	19,700	
Psychiatrists	16,300	
Phthisiologists (tuberculosis specialists)	23,600	
Dermato-venereologists	13,500	
Roentgenologists	26,400	
Specialists in physical culture	3,500	
Physicians of the public health and communicable diseases groups[c]	43,700	
Nonspecified and nonspecialized[d]	98,700	
Total physicians		644,600
Stomatologists[e]		45,600
Dentists[f]		51,600

Semiprofessional Personnel		
Feldshers	501,000	
Feldsher-midwives	79,800	
Midwives	231,700	
Assistants to public health physicians and epidemiologists	41,100	
Nurses	1,106,500	
Laboratory technicians	94,600	
X-ray technicians and X-ray laboratory technicians	27,100	
Dental technicians	27,600	
Disinfection instructors and disinfectors	78,900	
Nonspecified[g]	81,300	
Total semiprofessionals		2,269,600

Source: *Narodnoe Khoziaistvo v SSSR 1972: Statisticheskii Ezhegodnik* (Moscow: Statistika, 1972), pp. 685–686.

[a]Includes general practitioners, family physicians, physiotherapists, infectionists.

[b]Includes surgeons, traumatologists, orthopedists, oncologists (cancer specialists), and urologists.

[c]Includes public health physicians, epidemiologists, malarialogists, bacteriologists, helminthologists, and disinfectionists.

[d]Residual category, not given in Soviet tables, consisting of the difference between total number of physicians and total listed in the specialties.

[e]Graduates of a stomatological faculty of a medical institute, i.e., dentists or mouth specialists with a professional degree.

[f]Graduates of a secondary medical school, i.e., dentists with a semiprofessional education.

[g]Residual category, not given in Soviet tables, consisting of the differences between total number of semiprofessional personnel and total listed in the specialties.

Table 7-5
Number of Physicians in the United States and USSR, 1910–1970

Year	U.S.	USSR
1910	135,000	–
1913	–[a]	23,200
1950	219,997	236,900
1960	260,484	385,400
1970	340,000	577,300

Source: Mark Field, "American and Soviet Medical Manpower: Growth and Evolution, 1910-1970," *International Journal of Health Services*, 5, 3 (1975): 458.

[a]No data.

that meant the application and further strengthening of the industrial model of production in medicine. It was indeed the further strengthening of scienitfic medicine, the main pillar of medicine, i.e., "science should be and is the foundation of health care."[5]

Soviet medicine, then, was based primarily on (1) scientific, or what we in the United States call Flexnerian, medicine, and (2) the need for the health sector to respond to and support the needs of capital accumulation and industrialization, i.e., the division of medicine not only according to Flexnerian systemic categories related to medical or bodily systems (neurology, cardiology, etc.), but also according to the specific needs for the care of different sectors of the population (adults, mothers and children, and workers), and the different activities (therapy versus preventive and environmental medicine).

That political commitment to industrialization and specialization in medicine had many consequences, one being the increased importance within the Soviet system of the center of scientific and technological development in medicine, i.e., the hospital. The rationalization and efficiency of the system required that the hospital be considered the axis of the system.

Moreover, that same rationalization demanded and required increased centralization of hospital facilities. And in a country in which 70 percent of the hospitals have 200 beds (with 30 percent having more than 500), there still is a perceived need for (1) further expanding the hospital sector, (2) further centralizing that sector, and (3) considering that sector as the axis of the system. As Dr. Venediktov, present Deputy Director of the USSR Ministry of Health, indicates:

In the present broad programme for the construction of medical institutions, particular emphasis is being laid on large hospitals (with 1,000 or more beds), which will become major centres for specialized medical attention, ensuring the necessary combination of specialists and integrated medical care. Taking into account the nature of hospitals in the USSR and their particular role in the health system (not only therapeutic but prophylactic, organizational and methodological), this will make it possible to raise even higher the level of health care for the populace.[6]

That hospital orientation is also reflected in the increased number of physicians and other personnel working in the hospital as distinct from ambulatory care. For example, as presented in Table 7-6, while the number of physicians working in ambulatory care increased threefold from 1947 to 1968, the number of physicians working in hospital care increased fourfold over the same time period.

That political commitment to the industrialization of medicine and the consequent focus on hospitalization go side by side with an increased specialization of and in medicine, a specialization, incidentally, that is for the most part hospital-based. It is interesting to note that within that scheme, quality of production is synonymous with a solidly-based background in biomedical sciences and research skills. In the words of the current president of hospital-based academic medicine in this country—the Association of American Medical Colleges:

A clear priority is being given to improving the quality of the Soviet physician. The biomedical sciences are becoming more important factors in the educational process. The faculty is engaging in more research . . . the goal is to increase the percentage of medical students undertaking research from 30 percent to 80 percent over the next five years.[7]

We thus find in the Soviet Union, as we find in those societies that adopted the scientific or Flexnerian model of medicine, an increasing hospital-oriented specialization of medicine, with increasing numbers of physicians and other human resources working in secondary and tertiary care specialties, and a proportional decline both in terms of numbers and prestige of general and primary care specialists. In looking at the distribution of physicians by specialty, we find a more rapid increase in secondary and tertiary care specialists (such as surgeons, neurologists, psychiatrists), than in generalists or primary care physicians (such as pediatricians or obstetricians and gynecologists). That increased specialization leaves the generalist or primary care specialist as a "sorting clerk" within the system, as observed by J. Hogarth:

Table 7-6
Number of Physicians in the USSR, 1947–1968
(in thousands)

Year	Total	Ambulatory Care	Hospital Care
1947	139	99	40
1960	333	221	112
1968	495	330	165

Source: G.A. Popov, "Outpatient and Hospital Care Facilities," *Public Health Papers*, No. 43, (Geneva: World Health Organization, 1971), p. 57.

With increasing specialization the general practitioner tends to be cut off from the specialities. These comments are familiar in the pages of *The Lancet* and the *British Medical Journal*, yet they are also found in an article published in the official organ of the University of Health and the Medical Trade Union of the Soviet Union by a member of the Soviet Academy of Medical Sciences who goes on to suggest in terms again familiar to the Western reader that the process of differentiation of medical specialties does not mean that the general practitioner must become a mere sorting clerk.[8]

There is, then, a gradient of specialization that also produces a gradient of prestige and monetary rewards. Indeed, we saw in Chapter 4 how political commitment to capital accumulation via industrialization determined that hierarchicalization of labor. Similarly, the scheme of industrialization in medicine determined its hierarchicalization. As we can see in Table 7-7, showing the salary levels of different elements of the labor force, at the top of the health sector we find the researchers and academicians, with the top selected few possessing a doctorate of medical science, while at the bottom within the medical profession, we find the rural practitioner, and within the overall health labor force the unskilled service worker.

Table 7-7
Estimated Monthly Salaries Among Occupations Within and Outside the Health Labor Force
(in rubles)

Health Labor Force (1955-1965)			*Labor Force (1965)*
Doctor of Medical Science	600–800		
Managers and administrators of health institutions	120–200	150	Engineers and technicians
Heads of clinical and other departments	77–120		
Physicians working in urban areas	74–110		
Physicians working in rural areas	77–108	80	White-collar workers
		60	Agricultural workers
Feldshers, midwives, head nurses	50–70		
Other paraprofessionals	37–67		
Nonprofessionals	35–45		

Sources: Salaries of the health labor force adapted from Mark Field, *Soviet Specialized Medicine* (New York: The Free Press, 1967), pp. 129–130; and *Report of the United States Public Health Mission to the USSR*, 1957, p. 22. General labor force salaries based on T. Vadimov, *Socialist Principles of Payments According to Work* (Moscow, 1974), p. 75.

A Final Note on Hierarchicalization and Income Differentials

The income differentiation and hierarchicalization that are clear and apparent in today's Soviet Union, with the skilled worker and expert getting far more than the unskilled, are clearly contrary to the intentions of the founders of socialism. Indeed, Engels made it quite clear that the expert's knowledge was public and not private property and that, thus, the individual should not take immediate material advantage of possessing that knowledge. He indicated that "The cost of specialized qualifications is borne by society, and therefore the fruits, the greater value created by complex labor, belong to society. The worker himself has no right to claim higher wages."[9]

Actually, just after the October Revolution, the top Party members' salaries were only twice the minimum subsistence wage of the ordinary citizen. Many exceptions were made, particularly for the experts and technicians, to gain their loyalty. Indeed, Lenin indicated that:

Even then we were forced to retreat on a number of points. For example, in March and April 1918, one issue was whether to pay specialists salaries that corresponded not to socialist but to bourgeois relations of production, i.e., rates which were not justified by the difficulty or complexity of the work but which conformed to bourgeois custom and would have been appropriate in a bourgeois society. Originally there had been no intention to provide such exceptionally high rewards for specialists (in no way exceptional, of course, in terms of bourgeois standards)—this would have meant contravening several decrees issued at the end of 1917. But at the beginning of 1918 the party directed that we must take a step backward and accept a certain degree of "compromise" [this was the word used at the time].[10]

Actually, following the same rationale, it is interesting to note that the new socialist government in Cuba also gave very high salaries and rewards to the medical profession and other specialists to avoid their leaving the country.[11]

Still, it was clear to both the founders of socialism and the founders of the Soviet Union (as well as to the present Cuban leadership) that that situation of salary differentials was to be a provisional one. Instead, Stalin clearly formalized and strengthened those salary differentials, reflecting the hierarchicalization of labor that was previously described. According to Stalin, "The equalization of wages and salaries is a reactionary petit-bourgeois absurdity worthy of a primitive set of ascetics but not of a socialist society organized on Marxist lines."[12] Today, for instance, the income differentials among salary earners are in general higher in the USSR and the Eastern European countries than in the United States.[13]

Two specific examples where salary differentials are prominent are found in academia and government. In large academic institutions in the USSR, the ratio between the salary of a junior research worker who holds no degree and that of an academician in charge of a department is 1:15 to 1:20 (without counting fringe benefits), far more generous for the latter than the former; in the United States that difference is 1:5 to 1:7. Also, in government the usual ratio between the highest paid official and the lowest paid is 1:20 or even 1:30, while in the United States it is 1:10 to 1:15. Medvedev writes that when fringe benefits are counted, then differentials can rise to 1:50 or sometimes even 1:100.[14] And this six decades after the Soviet Revolution! The meaning of provisional is a very relative one indeed.

Class-ization of the Soviet Health Labor Force

Parallel to the just-described hierarchicalization of the health labor force, there has been a change in the social class and sex composition of the labor force that is worth explaining. Indeed, Stalin's reforms in university education (including medical education), in which prior academic performance and not social class origin was the criterion for an applicant's acceptance to university education, had an immediate and lasting impact on the social class composition of the professional occupations, including the medical profession. The children of professionals and white-collar families went from a minority to a majority position among medical students, i.e., they constituted the majority of university (including medical) students. Let me clarify here that academic performance was defined by the faculty of the medical teaching institutions, individuals who, besides having been trained in scientific medicine, belonged to the professional strata within the upper-middle class. These specific class and professional backgrounds of the faculty undoubtedly gave a class and professional bias to the meaning of academic performance.

Last but not least, let me also underline that the class composition of the medical student body also changed in those periods, as in Lenin's time, when a special policy had been established favoring children of the working class, or where, as in Lenin's and Khrushchev's time, special evening colleges had been established to enable adult workers to attend the medical schools in nonworking time.

Women as Producers of Health Services in the Soviet Union

Another change in the health labor force was the change in its sexual composition. Indeed, due to the great scarcity of males in Soviet society as a result of the losses sustained during World War II, among other factors, there was a massive feminization of the labor force and primarily of the social sectors, including health. Today, women, in the Soviet Union, as in the United States, constitute the majority of workers in the health labor force—85 percent in the USSR[15] and 87 percent in the U.S.[16] However, in analyzing and comparing the sex composition of the health labor force in both countries, large differences appear. In fact, while the overwhelming majority of the nonprofessional and paraprofessional categories are women in both countries, the large majority of professionals are women in the USSR and men in the United States. As shown in Figure 7-1, in the USSR, 85 percent of nonprofessionals, 99 percent of nurses, 85 percent of feldshers, 75 percent of physicians, and 50 percent of the top health administrators and managers are women. In the United States, the equivalent figures for nurses, physicians, and administrators are 97 percent, 7 percent, and 10 percent, respectively.[17] The largest differences, then, exist in what is usually referred to as "the top" in the health sector. Those differences first appeared after the 1917 October Revolution, as was discussed in Chapter 4, with the increased feminization of the medical profession, which reached a peak immediately after World War II when 76 percent of the physicians (excluding the military) were women. Since then, the percentage of women in the medical profession has been slowly declining, with 72 percent today being women. The percentage is likely to decline further since the number of male medical students has been rising steadily in the last decade, with 48 percent of the medical students in 1972 being men.

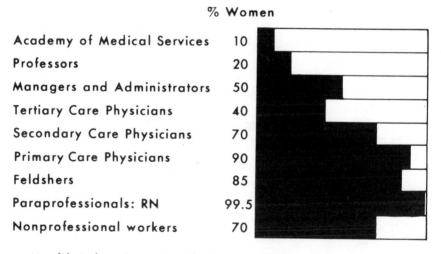

% Women

Academy of Medical Services	10
Professors	20
Managers and Administrators	50
Tertiary Care Physicians	40
Secondary Care Physicians	70
Primary Care Physicians	90
Feldshers	85
Paraprofessionals: RN	99.5
Nonprofessional workers	70

Health Labor Force Total: 85% women

Source: Adapted from M.D. Piradova, "The Role of Women in the Public Health Care System in the USSR," (Paper presented at the International Conference on Women in Health, Department of Health, Education and Welfare, Washington, D.C., 1975); *Yearbook for Labor Statistics, 1974* (Geneva: International Labour Organization, 1974); *Results of the 1970 All-Union Census: Occupational Distribution of the Population of the USSR* (Moscow: Central Statistical Administration, 1973); B. Danilov, "Soviet Health Services," *Moscow News*, No. 16 (April 1967):30; and personal visit to the Semaschko Institute, 1974.

Figure 7-1. Women in the USSR Health Labor Force, 1967-1974

Reasons for that feminization of medicine are many, and as usual, most of them are a response more to forces outside than from within the health sector, primarily to changes in the economic mode of production and changes in the labor force determined by these economic changes. Indeed, the political commitment to capital accumulation via the massive industrialization that characterized the period of industrialization, as described in Chapter 4, determined the priority given to the primary and secondary sectors of the economy over the tertiary ones. And in a labor force where (1) men were assumed to be more productive, and (2) a great shortage of men existed, the majority of men worked in the primary and secondary care sectors, and women worked primarily in the tertiary care sectors. Let me clarify here, however, that women did contribute dramatically to the primary and secondary sectors as well. Indeed, as shown previously, over 50 percent of the agricultural workers in the Soviet Union and 40 percent of the workers employed in the manufacturing, construction, transportation, and communication sectors have been and continue to be women.[18] Thus women have played an important role not only in the supportive sectors, such as health, where they constitute an overwhelming majority, but also in the productive sectors, where in some sectors, such as agriculture, they constitute a majority, while in other sectors they compose quite substantial minorities.

It can be postulated that another reason for the feminization of medicine was the prevalent ideology of the family in Soviet society, with the subsequent division of responsibilities within that unit and its subsequent mystique, i.e., women were supposed to be better physicians, nurses, and teachers because of the supporting characteristics of their personalities. The caring, motherly, and wifely functions thus became reflected in the social distribution of responsibilities, leading to the predominance of women in the supportive social sectors of the economy. It is interesting to add here, as a symbolic footnote, that Soviet physicians, although not the best paid among professionals, are today among the most respected and esteemed professionals. Indeed, in the only survey USSR published on people's attitudes toward professions, physicians ranked first among professionals, reflecting the importance that the population, in contrast to the economic leadership, may attribute to that caring function, particularly in times of distress and of need.[19]

The Different Degrees of Feminization of Medicine

The prestige of the Soviet medical profession varies, however, depending on the hierarchy within the labor force. Indeed, translating the priorities consequent to Flexnerian medicine, we previously stated that within the medical profession there exists a gradient of prestige, with academicians at the top and generalists and primary care physicians at the bottom. Within this gradient, women, although represented at all levels of the labor force, hold a smaller percentage of the top positions. For example, in Table 7-8, which presents the detailed sex composition among all medical professionals, we can see that

Table 7-8
Feminization of the Different Medical Specialties

Branch of Medicine	Percentage of Women
Pediatrician, obstetrician-gynecologist, cardio-rheumatologist, endocrinologist, laboratory doctor, bacteriologist	> 90%
Therapist, infectionist, ophthalmologist, hemotologist, dietician, physiotherapist	80 – 90%
Epidemiologist, neuropathologist, otolaryngologist, phthisiologist, stomatologist, remedial physical culture doctor, ECG doctor, gastroenterologist, doctor-statistician	70 – 80%
Oncologist, psychiatrist, roentgenologist, medically qualified sanitarian, nephrologist, doctor specializing in the health education of the population	60 – 70%
Cardiovascular surgeon, health care organizer, toxicologist, patho-anatomist	50 – 60%
Anesthesiologist-reanimator	> 40%
Surgeon, traumatologist-orthopedician, urologist, chest surgeon	30 – 40%

Source: M.D. Piradova, "The Role of Women in the Public Health Care System in the USSR," Paper presented at the International Conference on Women in Health, Department of Health, Education and Welfare, Washington, D.C., June, 1975.

women constitute the large majority among generalists and primary care specialists (primarily among pediatricians, of whom 93.3 percent are women), while they are a minority (although a sizable one) among tertiary care specialists; for example, 25 percent of all neurosurgeons are women. Let me emphasize, however, that even among tertiary care specialists, Soviet women are far better represented than women in the United States, where the percentage of women among neurosurgeons is less than 1 percent.

At another level of the health labor force, as shown in Figure 7-1, we find that women constitute over 50 percent of all the head administrators and managers of health institutions, yet they represent only a minority (although again a sizable minority) among professors, and a rather small minority among members of the National Academy of Medicine.

Why The Different Degrees of Feminization?

Different theories have been proposed to explain the varying degrees of feminization of the medical profession. One theory repeated by some feminist groups in our country is that the relatively lower prestige of the primary care specialists over the academicians and tertiary care specialists is due to the sex composition of both groups, with women being the majority among the former and men the majority among the latter. According to that interpretation, the lower prestige of generalists is because most of them are women. A historical review of this feminization, however, shows (as was discussed in Chapter 4) that this is an inaccurate interpretation of the past and present. Indeed, the relatively lower prestige of primary care physicians as compared to tertiary care specialists, for example, is primarily due to the Flexnerian interpretation of medicine, which explains that in all countries that have followed such a model, the same order of prestige and rewards appears, regardless of the sex composition of the different specialties. One could easily postulate that even if all physicians were women, the prestige differentials would remain practically the same.

Contrary to the theory of those feminists, the Soviet experience indicates that the lower prestige of the primary care specialty is not due to the preponderance of women in it, but rather the opposite. That is, Soviet women are stimulated and encouraged to enter the medical profession but, reflecting the overall predominance of men in the corridors of power in that society, women are encouraged to start with the lower and not the higher prestige jobs. It is basically an opening of opportunities in which both sexes, however dramatic the improvements women may have made, still do not have the same opportunities. In this respect, one could postulate that the perpetuation of woman's role in the family in Soviet society, where women are still considered to have supportive functions, is and will continue to deny full equality of opportunities to women.

One Final Note on the Feminization of Soviet Medicine

Any presentation of the situation of women in the health sector in the Soviet Union would not be complete without answering another point usually made by large sectors of the U.S. feminist movement, i.e., that socialism and capitalism are irrelevant categories in the solution of the "women's problem," since women in the Soviet Union (assumed to be a socialist country) are as discriminated against as women in the United States (assumed to be a capitalist one). Without discussing whether or not the Soviet Union is a socialist country, let me only emphasize the inaccuracy of the observation expressed in that statement. Indeed, the statistics presented in this and subsequent chapters speak for themselves. Women in the Soviet Union are far more active in the labor force, both at the top as well as at the bottom, than are women in the United States, showing a far broader spectrum of labor opportunities for women in the Soviet Union than in the United States. To deny this is tantamount to the vulgar anti-Sovietism that is so prevalent among large sectors of our media, including academia. The fact that women in the Soviet Union do not share equal opportunity with men does not deny that women have far, far greater opportunities in the Soviet Union than in the United States.

As do many other liberation campaigns, the Soviet experience shows that the seizure of state power by a working-class-based party is a necessary but not a sufficient condition to provide for the liberation of women. A continuous ideological and cultural revolution is required to break down not only the objective conditions of male supremacy, but the subjective ones as well. And this is particularly so in the liberation of women; surely, the longest march of them all.

Indeed, in Marxist terms the change of the infrastructure does not automatically create a parallel change in the superstructure or ideological apparatus. A dialectical relationship exists between both levels, whereby the absence of a continuous and steady interest in changing that ideology may determine the perpetuation of values and attitudes that created the set of former class and sex relations which sustained the previous infrastructure. This explains the need for a continuous cultural revolution whereby those values and attitudes can be questioned, eliminated, and their replication avoided. From the data presented, it seems that that continuous cultural revolution aimed at the liberation of Soviet women is, if presently existent, a slow one.

Still, the data presented in this chapter cannot be dismissed and speak for themselves. Soviet women have far more opportunities than women living in the capitalist world. And the same applies to most socialist countries. Of all the countries of the Americas—South, Central, or North—Cuba shows how socialism offers a better economic and ideological environment for the liberation of women than capitalism does.

8

The Function of State Intervention in the Soviet Health Sector

In trying to evaluate the Soviet central system of health planning, it has become common practice among Western scholars to (1) describe and study the wide differences in the availability of health resources among the Soviet republics, as well as among the urban and rural regions, and (2) show this disparity as an example of the failure and/or serious limitations of central planning, concluding that even the Soviet Union--that country assumed to be the paradigm of central planning—has altogether failed to solve the urban/rural disparities in the availability of care. American authors add, in a somewhat self-congratulatory tone, that the Soviet Union is in as bad a situation as we are. And, not infrequently, this apparent similarity is also used to prove the theory of convergence, according to which the Soviet Union and the United States are increasingly similar and destined to the same end.

Those authors, however, make two gross mistakes (one conceptual, the other methodological) which lead them unavoidably to the wrong conclusions. In assuming that central planning has failed to equally distribute the resources among urban and rural areas, they conceptually assume that equalization in the distribution of resources among rural and urban areas was and is a primary goal of central planning, and, in assuming that central planning has failed to distribute health resources equally and equitably, they assume that that equalization was a primary goal of the system of planning. As I will show, this was and is not the case. Moreover, this conceptual mistake seems to have been the result of using the prevalent method of analysis in health services research in Western sociology, i.e., empirical analysis of the tree—the health sector—without looking at the forest—the economic and political forces that shape not only the nature of the entire economic and political system but of the health sector as well. As I have indicated elsewhere,[1] to understand the function, distribution, and composition of the health sector (including, of course, its system of planning and regulation), we must analyze the economic and political forces outside the health sector. To do otherwise, to study and analyze the health sector in isolation from the economic system, is likely to lead to the most frequent conclusion of health services researchers: that the nature of the health sector is primarily determined by forces within the health sector itself. Contrary to that approach, I suggest that to understand the nature, composition, and distribution of health resources, we must go outside the health sector and study what social classes and groups in a given society have dominant influence on defining the functions of the health sector and on regulating the distribution of resources. In other words, in order to

81

understand the distribution of health resources, we must analyze what the dominant class in that society perceives the nature and functions of state intervention to be, and within it, the nature and functions of the health sector.

As shown in Chapter 4, the main functions of state intervention in the Soviet Union, as perceived by the top echelons of the Communist Party, were to legitimatize the system and to stimulate rapid capital accumulation via massive industrialization. From this, one may conclude that the two primary functions of the Soviet health sector were and are to support and contribute to that legitimization of the system and to capital accumulation.

The Health Sector as an Instrument of Legitimization: Inter-Republic Cohesion

A primary function of the Soviet state, or of any other state for that matter, is to provide the political and social cohesion that is required to assure and/or facilitate the citizenry's acceptance of the system. As part of that function, an important role of Soviet state intervention is to provide such cohesion among the fifteen republics of the Union. Considering the great diversity among those republics, which represent different cultures and histories, this is of primary importance. And one strategy, among others, to strengthen cohesion is to diminish the differentials in the availability of resources among republics. The central planning machinery in the health sector has, in this respect, successfully diminished inter-republic differences in the availability of resources. To realize the degree of that success, we must analyze the changes in the availability of resources during the last three decades. Here again is a point where most Western writers, in trying to evaluate inter-republic differences in the availability of resources, have focused on distribution at just one particular moment. And finding wide disparities in distribution, they conclude central planning has failed.

However, if one makes an analysis not only of a given moment, but of the historical trend over the past three decades, then one can see, as shown in Tables 8-1 and 8-2, how the inter-republic disparities in the availability of physicians as well as paramedical personnel have dramatically diminished throughout that period.

Table 8-1 shows not only a dramatic increase in the availability of physicians per republic in terms of the physician to population ratio, but also a decline in the inter-republic differentials of physician density. For example, while in 1940 the republic with the highest ratio of physicians to population (Georgia) had a ratio 3.2 times as high as the republic with the lowest (Tadjkistan), that ratio had decreased to 2.1 by 1970.

Table 8-2 presents a similar situation for paramedical personnel. And in both cases, for physicians as well as for paramedical personnel, the range of the ratios of availability of human resources declined substantially.

Table 8-1
Ratio of Physicians to Population by Soviet Republic
(per 10,000 population)

Republic	1940	1960	1965	1970	1971	1972
RSFSR	8.2	20.8	24.8	29.0	30.1	31.3
Ukraine	8.4	19.9	24.3	27.6	28.3	29.2
Byelorussia	5.7	16.4	21.8	25.8	26.7	27.7
Uzbekistan	4.7	13.9	17.0	20.1	21.0	22.1
Kazakhstan	4.3	14.0	18.7	21.8	22.9	24.3
Georgia	13.3	33.0	35.0	36.2	36.8	37.6
Azerbaijan	10.0	23.7	23.8	25.0	25.1	25.6
Lithuania	6.7	17.4	21.5	27.4	28.6	29.9
Moldavia	4.2	14.3	17.9	20.5	21.5	22.7
Latvia	13.2	26.4	31.2	35.6	36.2	36.7
Kirghizia	3.8	15.4	19.1	20.7	21.4	22.1
Tadjikistan	4.1	12.7	15.0	15.9	16.6	17.5
Armenia	7.5	24.0	26.7	28.8	29.4	30.5
Turkmenistan	7.6	18.7	21.2	21.4	21.9	22.5
Estonia	10.0	23.9	29.5	33.1	33.8	34.5
Total for entire USSR	7.9	20.0	23.9	27.4	28.3	29.4

Source: *Narodnoe Khoziaistvo v SSSR 1972: Statisticheskii Ezhegodnik*. (Moscow: Statistika, 1973), p. 684.

Table 8-2
Ratio of Paraprofessional Personnel to Population by Soviet Republic
(per 10,000 population)

Republic	1940	1960	1965	1970	1971	1972
RSFSR	26.1	67.7	77.0	92.8	94.9	97.5
Ukraine	24.1	63.9	72.8	86.6	88.9	91.0
Byelorussia	19.7	54.2	65.4	80.6	82.9	84.8
Uzbekistan	18.2	44.1	51.8	64.8	67.4	69.7
Kazakhstan	18.6	57.1	63.5	80.1	82.6	84.2
Georgia	25.6	73.3	82.3	91.2	92.9	94.0
Azerbaijan	22.5	65.6	67.4	76.1	76.9	78.1
Lithuania	6.9	53.1	64.7	78.0	80.6	82.5
Moldavia	9.8	54.0	65.0	77.3	78.8	80.2
Latvia	18.7	71.8	83.5	92.6	94.3	96.1
Kirghizia	16.1	48.8	58.8	72.1	73.5	74.4
Tadjikistan	17.0	39.7	42.4	51.5	55.8	56.2
Armenia	17.1	59.5	66.0	70.2	70.7	73.1
Turkmenistan	35.5	65.5	68.6	72.3	71.8	72.6
Estonia	14.1	77.5	87.2	93.7	94.9	95.7
Total for entire USSR	24.0	64.2	72.8	87.1	89.1	91.3

Source: *Narodnoe Khoziaistvo v SSSR 1972: Statisticheskii Ezhegodnik*, (Moscow: Statistika, 1973), p. 687.

In the United States, however, the situation is precisely the opposite. Indeed, we find that not only has the density of physicians per population in the low density states been declining in the last decades, but the density differentials between the lowest and highest density states have been increasing. It is difficult to conclude from those figures that (1) the system of central planning has failed in reducing inter-republic density differentials, an important goal in the legitimization of the central planning intervention, and that (2) maldistribution of resources in the USSR and the United States is either similar or the same.

The Health Sector as an Instrument of Industrialization:
The Urbanization of Resources

Besides the previously-mentioned goal of the legitimization of the system, there is an additional goal of state intervention, which has been and is to stimulate capital accumulation and massive industrialization. Accordingly, another important goal of the health sector (and its central planning machinery), in addition to the goal of legitimization, is one of supporting and assisting that industrialization.[a] Consequent to the second objective, we find in the Soviet Union an increased deployment of human health resources to the industrial and urban areas, following a massive program of both industrialization and urbanization as was defined in Chapter 4. Moreover, the political commitment to massive industrialization has been accompanied by the strengthening of those forces within medicine that further stimulated its urbanization.[b] These forces are: (1) the previously-discussed implementation of the Flexnerian model in medicine with emphasis on systemic body orientation and hospital-based specialization; (2) the university reforms, also previously discussed, which gave priority in medical school acceptance to expertise and merit over social class and regional origin; and (3) the subsequent emphasis on the technologization and depoliticization of the expert, the professional of medicine. Indeed, the Stalinist and Khrushchevian eras reversed the Leninist expression "better red than expert" to "better expert than red." Actually, reflecting that depolitization, the political studies of Marxism, Leninism, and collectivism were and are taught mechanically and, according to an American observer, "the instruction [of Marxism-Leninism] is not always taken seriously by the students, any more than are the compulsory courses in 'military sciences' provided in many American universities."[2]

---

[a]It should be emphasized that these two goals, generating two different types of forces, are interrelated—on occasion in conflict with each other, and other times complementary. Indeed, as I will show later, the force for inter-republic equalization may conflict with the higher needs of industrialization.

[b]By urbanization of medicine, I mean the increased deployment of health resources to urban areas.

These three forces determined that technology, organizational management and specialization were and are the main ingredients of the new development in the Soviet health system. In the words of one of its present leaders: "The improvement of the quality of prophylactic and therapeutic work first and foremost depends on the technical equipment of the health care establishments, on the perfection of the organizational forms, providing optimum conditions for work and creative activities for every specialist."[3] Altogether, these three forces—the Flexnerianization of medicine, white-collarization and urbanization of medical students, and the technologization and depoliticization emphasized by the medical curriculum and medical studies—determined both the hospital orientation and specialization of medicine, and further strengthened the urban orientation of the health sector that went side by side with the supportive role of that sector to the process of industrialization, graphically presented in Figure 8-1.

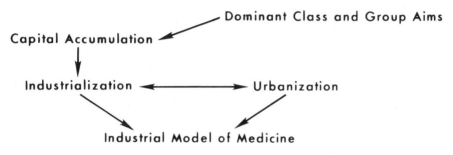

Industrial Model of Medicine

(1) Flexnerian Scientific Medicine

(2) Hospital-Oriented Specialization

(3) White Collarization and Urbanization
of Medical Students

(4) Technologicalization and Depoliticalization
of Medical Students and Medicine

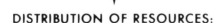

DISTRIBUTION OF RESOURCES:

Toward Urban and Wealthy Areas

Toward Hospital-Based Specialties

Away from Rural and Poor Areas

Away from Ambulatory Care

Figure 8-1. The Relationship among Different Forces Towards the Urbanization of Medicine

In summary, then, industrialization and massive urbanization determined the rapid deployment of human health resources to the urban areas, a tendency which was further strengthened by the three forces outlined above. That tendency is tentatively reflected in Soviet statistics. As shown in Table 8-3, the total number of personnel on the payroll of the Ministry of Health deployed in the urban areas has grown faster than that in rural areas.

Regarding physicians, Table 8-4 presents the ratio of physicians per 10,000 population in urban and rural areas in each republic in 1961, showing marked

Table 8-3

Total Number of Medical Workers on the Payroll of the Ministry of Health, 1950-1956

Year	In Cities	In Rural Areas	Total
1950	415,300	232,400	647,700
1955	563,500	281,500	845,000
1956	625,300	304,300	929,600

Source: *The Report of the United States Health Mission to the Union of Soviet Socialist Republics, August 13 to September 14, 1957* (Washington, D.C.: U.S. Government Printing Office, 1959), p. 23.

Table 8-4

Ratio of Full-Time Physicians in Clinical-Preventive Service by Soviet Republic, 1961

(per 10,000 population)

Republic	Urban Population	Rural Population	Total Population
RSFSR	27.3-	9.4	19.4
Ukraine	27.6	10.5	18.9
Byelorussia	27.2	11.0	16.7
Uzbekistan	28.8	8.2	15.4
Kazakhstan	24.3	8.5	15.5
Georgia	34.0	13.5	22.8
Azerbaijan	31.4	8.6	19.9
Lithuania	30.1	12.0	19.4
Moldavia	33.7	8.8	14.8
Latvia	29.4	17.1	24.2
Kirghizia	24.7	10.4	15.7
Tadjikistan	28.0	7.2	14.4
Armenia	29.0	10.9	20.4
Turkmenistan	29.6	8.5	18.6
Estonia	30.9	15.1	24.4
Total for entire USSR	27.6	9.8	18.8

Source: G.A. Popov, "The Problem of Posting and Utilizing Physicians," *Sovetskoe Zdravookhranenie*, No. 10 (1962): 26-33. (In Russian)

differences among those areas. Needless to say, these statistics underrepresent the differences within urban areas. For example, in 1972, Moscow and Leningrad had 76 and 71 physicians per 10,000 inhabitants respectively, compared with the national average for that year of 28.3. It is interesting to note that this increased deployment of human resources to the urban areas appears more clearly when, instead of analyzing large political and demographic units like the republics, one studies the changes of physician distribution by smaller units, regions, or oblasts, comparing changes of the physician/population ratio with the changes in the degree of urbanization during the period 1940-1970. One can see that the oblasts which urbanized ·more rapidly were also the ones having a faster growth in the physician/population ratio, indicating a more rapid centralization and urbanization of human health resources than found in oblasts with slower urban growth.

For example, Figures 8-2 and 8-3 (based on the Appendix) show the direct correlation between changes in the percentage of urbanization in each oblast and changes for the same time period in the number of physicians per 10,000 population.

The same picture appears for larger political and demographic units, such as in the major census regions. Indeed, we can see from Table 8-5 how those major census regions (e.g., Central and Northern Caucasus) that urbanized more rapidly in the period 1956-1971, also had higher increases in the physician/population ratio.

Is There a Substitution Effect Between Physicians and Feldshers?

One final note worth emphasizing is that when comparing Tables 8-1 and 8-2, showing physician and paramedical personnel densities in the fifteen republics, one can see that the higher density of paramedical personnel tends to be in those republics that have a higher degree of urbanization and a higher density of physicians as well. Also, if we compare the number of physicians and para-medical personnel by regional census districts, as shown in Table 8-6, we can see that here again, those regional districts have a higher number of physicians (which are also the districts with a larger degree of urbanization), are also the ones that have a larger number of paramedical personnel.

Since a large percentage of paramedical personnel are either feldshers or midwives, these figures would seem to suggest that there is no substitution effect between physicians and feldshers and/or midwives over regional districts or republics. Thus, the frequently quoted substitution of feldshers "covering" the understaffed areas must occur, if it occurs, at a far more disaggregate level, probably within the oblasts. The only data available would seem to indicate that at least at the republic and regional district levels, the lower the number of physicians available, the lower the number of paramedical personnel.

88

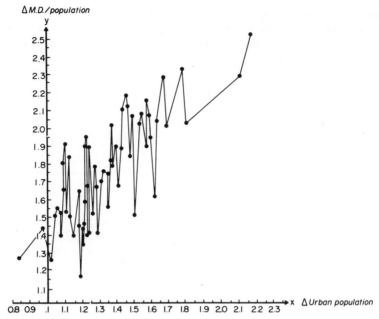

Figure 8–2. Relationship between Changes in Urbanization and Changes in the Availability of Physician per Population (10,000 pop.) by Soviet Oblasts, 1959–1971.

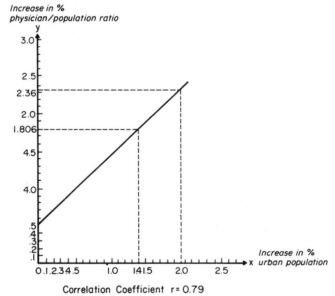

Correlation Coefficient r = 0.79

Figure 8–3. Relationship between Increases in Phys/Pop. Ratio and Increases in Urban Population by Soviet Oblasts, 1957–1971.

Table 8-5

Percentage of Urban Population and Physicians Per 10,000 Population by USSR Census Region, 1956 and 1971

Census Region	Percentage of Urban Population		Physicians/10,000 Population	
	1956	1971	1956	1971
Northern Region	40	_a	12.9	–
Northwest Region	71	75	31.9	41.2
Central Region	44	73	17.8	39.6
Pavolskii Region	47	59	19.4	26.3
Northern Caucasus Region	37	51	18.1	27.9
Urals Region	55	71	14.1	23.8
West Siberian Region	44	63	12.5	25.9
South Siberian Region	46	64	14.0	23.8
Far Eastern Siberian Region	67	73	18.0	32.1
Volga Vyatskii Region	–	55	–	23.3
Central Chernozemnye Region	–	43	–	21.4

Sources: *Narodnoe Khaziaistvo v RSFSR, 1957: Statisticheski Sbornik* (Moscow: Gosudarstvenoe Statisticheskoe Izdatelstvo, 1957), and *Narodnoe Khaziaistvo v RSFSR, 1971: Statisticheskii Ezhegodnik* (Moscow: Statistika, 1972).

[a]No data.

Table 8-6

Numbers of Physicians and Paraprofessional Personnel in the USSR by Census Region, 1940 and 1955

Census Region	Number of Physicians (in thousands)		Number of Paraprofessional Personnel (in thousands)	
	1940	1955	1940	1955
Northern Region	1.6	4.1	9.3	18.6
Northwest Region	13.6	23.5	32.0	53.8
Central Region	40.1	77.6	123.9	225.5
Pavolskii Region	7.9	19.4	24.6	54.7
Northern Caucasus Region	9.2	20.0	25.2	51.0
Urals Region	7.0	22.1	34.8	76.2
West Siberian Region	4.9	14.9	21.4	49.9
South Siberian Region	3.7	9.2	12.4	27.6
Far Eastern Siberian Region	2.8	7.8	6.8	21.6

Source: *Narodnoe Khaziaistvo v RSFSR, 1957: Statisticheski Sbornik* (Moscow:Gosudarstvenoe Staticheskoe Izdatelstvo, 1957).

The Decision-Making, Planning, and Regulatory Machinery in the Soviet Health System

Since Stalin's 1936 Constitution, there have been three main branches in the Soviet state system: the political, the legislative, and the governmental branches, as outlined in Table 9-1.

Let me now briefly summarize the three main branches, as formally described by the official sources of the Soviet Union. The decision-making branch is the Communist Party of the Soviet Union (CPSU), whose function is to direct and provide the main policy for the operation of all organs of the state. The legislative branch includes the Soviet structure and has the function of legislating within the goals, objectives, and boundaries defined by the CPSU. And the governmental branch includes the ministries and departments in charge of implementing that legislation.

The Party

The CPSU, the most important decision-making body in the USSR, operates in theory according to the principles of democratic centralism, which under Party rules means:

1. election of all leading Party bodies, from the lowest to the highest;
2. periodic reports of Party bodies to their Party organizations and to higher bodies;
3. strict Party discipline and subordination of the minority to the majority; and
4. the decisions of higher Party bodies are obligatory for lower bodies.[1]

According to the first principle, the basic units, cells or organizational bodies, based for the most part in the working place (e.g., factories or hospitals), elect the rayon or district committee of the Party, which elects the oblast committee, which elects the republican committee, which elects the Congress of the CPSU (the Party's supreme body), which elects the Central Committee, which elects the Politburo, which elects the Secretary General. The Congress of the Party meets once every four years. During this period, the maximum authority is vested in the Central Committee, led by the Secretary General.[a] Its enormous centralized power is ensured by the following mechanisms:

---

[a]The Central Committee is divided into several commissions, one of them on Health and Social Welfare.

Table 9-1
The Soviet State System

Party (Political)	Parliament (Legislative)	Bureaucracy (Government)
Politburo	Presidium	Cabinet
General Secretary	President	Premier
Central Committee	Supreme Soviet	Council of Ministers
Party Structure	Parliamentary Structure	Ministerial Structure
Bodies and Cells in Factories, Health Institutions, etc.	Soviets in Republics, Oblasts, Towns, and Villages	Finance, Education, Health, etc.

1. strict discipline of the Party membership;
2. its decisions are binding at all levels of the Party and of the Soviet Government;
3. all new memberships to the Party, all leading positions in government, all heads of enterprises, and all newspaper editors must be approved by the Central Committee of the Party.[2]

It is interesting to note that this strong centralism originated in the clandestine activities of the Bolshevik Party, described and discussed in Chapter 2. Centralized power was later maintained since it was considered to be the best mechanism for leading a backward country subject to the hostility of most other countries towards what was perceived as the most important goal of the Soviet state at that time—namely, capital accumulation via massive industrialization. Again, it is also worth underlining that measures that had been taken as provisional ones (the authority of the Central Committee of the Party to approve all Party positions and positions of authority, and the prohibition of factions) were, in Lenin's time, supposed to be that and not become normal features of the Party.[3]

Also worth stressing is that parallel to the commitment to massive industrialization, there was a substantial change in the composition of the Party from an initial working class predominance during Lenin's era, to the current white-collar predominance. In 1968, for example, although the Soviet population as a whole was made up of 55 percent manual workers, 20 percent white-collar or nonmanual workers, and 25 percent peasants and agricultural workers, these sectors constituted 39 percent, 45 percent, and 16 percent respectively of CPSU membership.[4] Also of interest is the fact that white-collar workers predominate in the Congress of the Party and in the Politburo. The top-level bureaucracy, estimated to comprise only 2.1 percent of total Party membership, represented 40 percent of the Congress delegates and 81 percent of the full membership of the Central Committee.[5] With regard to women, in 1968 they represented 21 percent of Party membership, 2.6 percent of the Central Committee, and were not represented at all in the Politburo.[6]

The Parliament or Supreme Soviet

The Supreme Soviet is composed of two houses. One is the Soviet of the Union, whose members are elected by the population, with one deputy per approximately 300,000 inhabitants. The second house is the Soviet of Nationalities, whose members are elected primarily by the Republican Soviets. Both houses have equal legislative rights and several committees, one of which is on Health and Social Welfare. The Supreme Soviet meets twice yearly, with meetings lasting from three to five days in which it approves or disapproves the legislation prepared by either the Presidium (thirty-seven members elected by the Supreme Soviet), the Cabinet, or special ad hoc commissions. Out of session, authority resides in the Presidium. The Supreme Soviet is comprised of 26.6 percent factory workers; 19.4 percent collective farmers; 34 percent government, Party, or union employees; and 16.2 percent other white-collar workers. Twenty-eight percent of its members are women—more, it is claimed, than the total number of women elected to all parliaments in Western countries. At local levels such as at the town Soviets, workers and peasants form the majority, with women representing 42 percent of the members of the local Soviets.

The Council of Ministers

The Council of Ministers (or Cabinet) appears to be the actual executive branch of the Soviet government. Its members are elected by the Supreme Soviet and include all the heads (Ministers) from every branch of government and special agencies or boards, such as the USSR State Bank Board, the Central Statistical Board, and others. The Cabinet is composed of eighty members, one of whom is the Minister of Health.

The Ministry of Health

This ministry is the top planning and regulatory body in the health sector, as was presented in Chapter 6, whose normative functions are primarily delegated to the Semaschko Institute. This institute is one of fifteen institutes of the Academy of Sciences, the Academy being roughly equivalent to our National Science Foundation. Within the Academy, the Semaschko Institute is the central agency for research (but not development) in the planning, organization, delivery, and funding of health services in the USSR; it is a body similar to former Senator Beall's (Rep.-Md.) proposed National Institute of Health Care. The Institute maintains a staff that includes approximately 300 full-time professionals advised by a large number of advisory councils which assist them in the development of their functions.

The full-time professionals and advisory councils of the Semaschko Institute are grouped into four main divisions: planning, statistics, management and organization, and international health. These advisory councils are extremely important within the health planning structure at the federal level. In the planning division—the division within the Semaschko Institute responsible for preparing the norms and standards in the Soviet Union for manpower development and also the estimates for the number, type, and location of specialists and training posts—members of the advisory councils are grouped according to medical specialties, which include the chiefs of the leading departments of Moscow's teaching institutions. Actually, the members of these advisory councils are the "prima donnas" of Soviet academic medicine, and approximately 10 percent are women. The councils, established in the period 1967-1970, advise the senior staff of the Semaschko Institute in their preparation of estimates of required human resources. These full-time professionals are roughly equivalent to our medical care researchers and administrators. For them, to work at the Semaschko Institute is the dream of their career. Approximately 20 percent of the professionals are women.

The top authority of the Semaschko Institute, both academically and administratively, is the Scientific Council, comprised of all the heads of the departments and divisions of the Institute. After their candidacy has been approved by the Executive Committee of the Communist Party of the Semaschko Institute, these department heads are elected by secret ballot by the full-time senior staff. Approximately 15 percent of the members of the Scientific Council are women.

Within the normative system, one is most impressed by the power of the expert. In fact, the overall value given to industrialization, specialization, and expertise has in turn given considerable power to the expert or technician, which in the health sector means the physician, especially the academic one. Indeed, we saw how physicians (primarily surgeons) were and are the heads and directors of all health institutions (with the hygienists as subdirectors). And within that structure, we also saw how the chiefs of the clinical departments of regional hospitals were also the regional heads for the provision of health services. This professional and academic dominance is also evident in the top planning agencies, such as the Ministry of Health and the Semaschko Institute, where academic medicine holds most important positions, either as staff or in a consultant relationship. Indeed, it is my impression that:

1. not unlike our National Institutes of Health, there is a strong formal—and, apparently, informal—relationship between members of the top echelons

of the Semaschko Institute and the leading figures in the academic medical establishment; and

2. the entire planning machinery of the health sector, including manpower planning, seems to rely very heavily on what are usually referred to as "laws of scientific development," i.e., laws defined by experts and scientists. The scientist or expert defines the norms and standards in almost every area of endeavor, the scientists and experts in the health sector being academic medicine and medical care professionals.

The Different Stages in the Planning Process

Within the structure that I have just described, let us analyze who decides, who implements, what information is used, how frequently the allocations of resources are revised, and what sanctions are used (see Figure 9-1 for a summary graph of this structure).

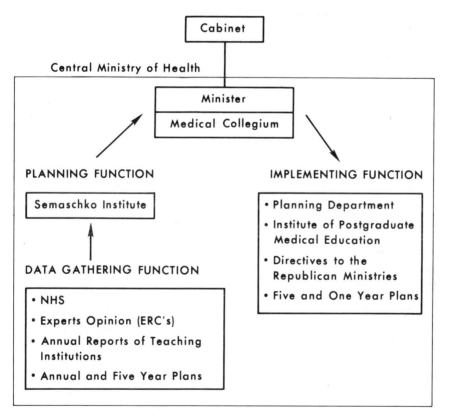

Figure 9-1. Decision-Making Function

Who Decides?

The top administrative authority within the Ministry of Health is the Minister, a member of the Cabinet. He is currently a surgeon and professor of surgery who combines his surgical duties—two mornings a week—with his administrative and political responsibilities. He may be one of the few ministers of health in the world who combines token clinical work with administration. My impression of this almost unique situation is that it serves a public relations purpose in that it may be a concession to the academic and clinical medical groups to make them feel that "one of them" is at the top. Under the Minister are four Vice Ministers who serve as full-time administrators. The Minister's authority, as in the case of any Cabinet member, is delegated from the Executive Committee of the Communist Party.

Advising the Minister of Health is the all-powerful Medical Collegium of the Ministry, a thirty-member council whose membership includes the four Vice Ministers, the chiefs of the departments and divisions of the Ministry, representatives of the trade unions and of the Communist Party of the Ministry, and representatives of academic medicine. The Minister chairs the Medical Collegium when it is in session. The power of the Medical Collegium is reflected in the fact that the advice it gives is very rarely, if ever, not accepted by the Minister. Five percent of the members of the Collegium are women.

Among other matters, the Director of the Semaschko Institute advises the Medical Collegium on the number of graduates and postgraduate trainees and training programs required for each republic and for the entire USSR. His advice has been, in the past, almost automatically accepted and converted into national policy. Recently, however, there has been some questioning of the overall quantity of the health resources said to be required by the Director of the Semaschko Institute, and his estimates have sometimes been considered too high.

What Information Is Used?

The Semaschko Institute bases its estimates of required numbers, types, and location of trainees and training programs on the following sources:

1. the annual reports of the republics' Ministries of Health which indicate the demand for new specialists and the availability of new medical graduates. The administration of medical undergraduate education is the responsibility of the Ministries of Health of the republics. All medical education, incidentally, is the responsibility of the Ministries of Health, not of the Ministries of Education;
2. the National Health Survey (NHS), a voluminous survey started in 1965, that includes (a) a household survey covering 4 million people which inquires

into perceived morbidity and utilization of health services, (b) a health screening survey, and (c) an institutional survey covering 1,800 delivery and teaching institutions which measures the productivity of those institutions. This NHS is run by the statistical group of the Semaschko Institute;

3. reports from Expert Review Committees (ERCs) which present evaluations of the type and quality of care provided by the health delivery and teaching institutions. These committees serve a function somewhat similar to the assigned function of the Professional Standards Review Organizations in the United States and check on the quality of care provided at the republic and local levels. The experts are leading medical academicians on leaves of absence from their own institutions who work for a period of one year on these committees, setting up the appropriate norms and standards of care for those areas. The Semaschko Institute, which appoints the committees (a total of twenty for the entire USSR), relies very heavily on them for its normative functions. It is worth emphasizing that norms and standards of care vary from republic to republic.

How Frequently Are the Allocations Revised?

The number and location of trainees and training programs as well as the number of job openings are reviewed annually as part of the cyclical planning process. These numbers and locations are estimated in the medium-term (five-year) and long-term (ten-year) plans. The types of trainees are estimated only on occasion, e.g., when new types of personnel are required.

How Are Policies Implemented?

The implementation of policies related to the planning and regulation of human health resources, as well as to any other policies in the health sector, is carried out from the Ministry of Health downwards. *In other words, decisions made by the Ministry of Health are binding on any lower administrative body in the health sector.*

The mechanisms of this implementation are:

1. control of the republican and oblast budgets, since most of the health sector is funded with central government funds;
2. nationwide norms and standards which are defined and prepared by the central government;
3. the concentration of administrative power, by which the decision of a superior administrative authority obliges all inferior ones;

4. the concentration of political power in the top leadership of the Communist Party, with a large number of the administrators in the health sector being members of the Party.

Due to the importance of these mechanisms, let me explain each one in more detail.

Budgeting as a Mechanism of Control

The overall gross national income of 1,166 billion rubles was disbursed in 1970 as indicated in Table 9-2.[7] In distributing the national income, it is estimated that 68.6 billion rubles, or 280 rubles per person, were allocated for public consumption, including free education, grants, pensions, development of physical culture and sport, accommodation in sanitoria and rest homes, national health services and other social benefits.[8] From that distribution, the total expenditures on health services in 1970 were equivalent to 65 rubles, 67 kopecks per person, including 37 rubles, 57 kopecks per person taken directly from the National Ministry of Health's budget. The balance came from health activities in other ministries (e.g., Defense) and from the republican, oblast, and local authorities.

Table 9-2
Expenditures of National Income, 1970
(in billions of rubles)

Salaries and payment for workers, employees, and collective farm workers	518
Education, health, culture	199
Income maintenance of people unable to work and scholarships to students	80
New capital investments	62
Development of science	41
Production savings and increases in stocks of goods and materials	186
Defense	80

Source: Adapted from D. Venediktov, "Union of Soviet Socialist Republics," in I. Douglas-Wilson and G. McLachlan (eds.), *Health Service Prospects* (Boston: Little, Brown and Co., 1973), p. 232.

The National Ministry of Health covers the funds for most of the operating expenditures of the health sector, and most of the capital investments for the eighty-two medical schools, nine university medical faculties, and thirteen institutes for postgraduate training. Capital investments for the other health institutions, including the oblast hospitals where most of the training of paramedical personnel takes place, are raised by the republics, and primarily by the local and regional Soviets. Also, the national government provides additional grants to the republics to assist them in the construction and/or expansion of facilities when deemed necessary.

In summary, then, we can see that nearly all the operating and large amounts of capital expenditures are controlled by the central government, which allows for a measure of central control that is used to implement the five- and one-year plans, including health services plans. The control over the operating and capital expenditures of the professional medical teaching institutions, and of the operating expenditures of the paraprofessional medical teaching institutions (with considerable leverage there as well with capital expenditures), gives enormous power to the central Ministry of Health over the production of human resources, exercised through the budgetary control which is approved every one and five years, according to the one- and five-year plans.

Similarly, the control that the central Health Ministry has over all budgeted positions of the majority of health institutions in the Soviet Union gives overwhelming control to that Ministry over the overall distribution of human health resources in that country. It is worth underlining that although the central Ministry has the power to control the overall distribution of human health resources through its direct control of the republic, oblast, and district budgets, still, most of that control is exercised indirectly via the establishment of norms and standards adapted to the republic, oblast, and district needs. Indeed, the overall central control over the budget is not exerted at the local institutional level. Rather, each superior administrative level approves the budget of the level immediately beneath itself, so that the local budget is approved by the oblast authority, the oblast budget is approved by the republic authority, and the republic budget is approved by the central authority. At each level, however, approval is based upon the guidelines made explicit by the norms and standards prepared by the central Ministry. Figure 9-2 presents a summary of the mechanism of control over the production and distribution of resources via budget control.

The Centralization of the Planning Process

Figure 9-3 shows the procedures for the preparation and approval of the National Health Plan of the USSR. In summary, we can see how (1) the outlines for preparing both the one- and five-year plans (including the plan's norms and

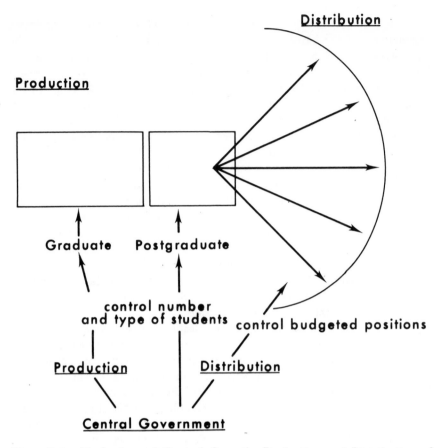

Figure 9-2. Mechanism of Control Over the Production and Distribution of Resources

standards move from the top to the bottom, and (2) final approval also runs from the top to the bottom, while (3) the preparation of the plans follows an inverse line, from the bottom to the top. This procedure reflects the overall political and administrative principle that *every superior decision binds all other lower authorities*. This gives the first and final administrative power to the central Ministry of Health, which also controls the normative functions described previously.

Let me quote extensively from a WHO report on National Health Planning that briefly summarizes all the planning processes:

Preparation of the health plan is begun at the medical establishments of the municipal and rayon health departments, on the basis of the guidelines received from Gosplan and the norms and standards laid down by the Ministry of

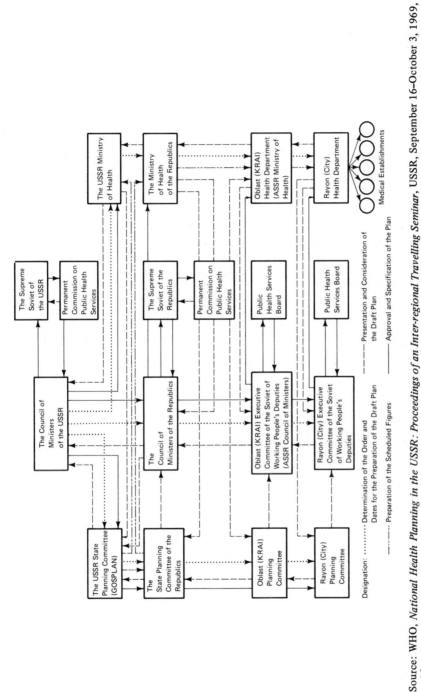

Source: WHO, *National Health Planning in the USSR: Proceedings of an Inter-regional Travelling Seminar*, USSR, September 16–October 3, 1969, p. 16.

Figure 9–3. Procedure for the Preparation and Approval of the National Health Plan in the USSR

Health of the USSR. The plans worked out are scrutinized by experts and thoroughly discussed by the appropriate planning committees. They are also carefully examined by the executive committee of the soviet of workers' deputies and the public health services board, and then submitted to the health department and planning committee of the oblast.

At the oblast level, the plans are examined and co-ordinated by the oblast health department and discussed with the oblast planning committee, the financial, manpower and other resources of the oblast being taken into account. In addition, the oblast planning committee is responsible for the co-ordination of the health plan with the plans for the other sectors of the economy, again from the point of view of the resources available. The plans are reexamined by the public health services board, and after they have been approved by the oblast executive committee of the soviet of workers' deputies, are forwarded to the Ministry of Health and State Planning Committee of the constituent republic concerned.

The plans received from the oblasts are very thoroughly examined at the constituent republic level. The examination is carried out by a special planning council, made up of representatives of the Ministry of Health of the republic, taken from planning units, research institutes and faculties of medicine, and of the Academy of Sciences. This council analyses the morbidity data, studies the manpower and financial requirements, and outlines measures to reduce the morbidity and mortality due to diseases of particular importance and to develop the system of health services. The draft plan is then discussed with the chairmen of the various oblast planning committees, the financial resources of the oblasts and the republic being taken into account. The necessary corrections to the plan are made, the need to develop certain oblasts, rayons or cities being borne in mind. The health plan is then co-ordinated with the plans for the other sectors of the economy. Thus the development of the health services is fitted into the planned economic and social development.

The plan is then submitted to the Council of Ministers of the republic and, after approval by the council, forwarded to the Ministry of Health and State Planning Committee of the USSR.

The Council of Ministers of the USSR states its opinions, approves the plan, and submits it to the Supreme Soviet of the USSR which, on the recommendation of the permanent commission on health services, accepts the plan. It then has the force of law, and is returned to the Government for implementation. It is subsequently forwarded to the lower administrative authorities where, after further detailed development, it is approved by the Supreme Soviets of the constituent republics and the various soviets of workers' deputies.[9]

The Political Centralization of the Party: A Final Note on the Theory of Convergence

Although administrative authority is centralized in the Ministry of Health, and final legislative authority is centralized in the Presidium of the Supreme Soviet, the final and most important authority resides in the Central Committee of the Party and the Politburo. This has great importance in the implementation of the one- and five-year plans since the administrative machinery is guided, supervised, and directed by the political one. Moreover, there is an interlinkage between the administrative and the political machinery that greatly facilitates those functions. For example, in 1964, all ministers and vice ministers of the health sector (both at the central and republican levels), 50 percent of all the heads of health institutions, and 20 percent of all physicians were members of the Party.[10] This situation causes the administrative and technocratic structure to be largely dependent on the political one which, as described earlier, is highly centralized, allowing and determining a very strong direction for health policies in the USSR.

Although, from visits to the different institutions and from a study of the formal structures, one may get the impression that, in the normal daily activities, the administrators are the ones who have more power in running the system, in actual practice, the ones who have the final say in overall matters of policy are the members of the Party and ultimately the top echelons of the Party. This point is of great importance since most of those Western scholars who tend to believe in the theory of convergence of socialist and capitalist systems assume that in both countries, the managers, administrators, and technocrats are the ones on the top, and constitute a "new class," which has replaced, as the controllers of the system, the "working class" in the socialist system and the "capitalist class" in the capitalist one. Indeed, in the words of one of its most successful popularizers,

Such reflection on the future should also emphasize the convergent tendencies of industrial societies, *however different their popular or ideological billing*, [emphasis mine] the convergence being to a roughly similar design for organization and planning . . . Convergence begins with modern large-scale production, with heavy requirements of capital, sophisticated technology, and, as a prime consequence, elaborate organization.[11]

But an analysis of the element of decision-making outside and within the health sector in the Soviet Union clearly shows that however powerful the planning technocrats and medical academicians may be in their normative function, and however powerful the administrators and the medical profession (especially academic medicine) may be in their administrative function, both planning and administrative functions are still subservient to a higher function—the decision-making function—and to a higher power—the power of the Party and especially of its Central Committee. And although those central bodies and that Party may delegate their powers to the planners and administrators, as indeed they do, still the latter power is primarily a delegated one. And when a conflict appears, as it does on occasion, there is no doubt who holds the final and foremost power, i.e., the top echelons of the Party.

In summary, there are elements of similarity, both within and outside medicine, between the United States and the USSR. And those elements translate a similar commitment in both societies to capital accumulation as the first objective, with concomitant and consequent mass industrialization and specialization and hierarchicalization of labor. But those processes of industrialization respond to the needs of different constituencies, i.e., the capitalist class in the United States and the dominant class in the USSR, the top echelons of the Party.[12] And it is that centralization of power (which, in the case of the USSR, is unprecedented and well-known) which is the one that determines that industrialization and not, as Illich and others postulate, vice versa. The managers in both societies are again answerable to a higher level: the one of the dominant class. And, as the empirical information presented here shows, this applies to the health sector as well.

10 Epilogue: The Nature of the Soviet Union and Its Medicine

In the preceding chapters, I have analyzed some of the different forces that determined the highly centralized nature of the Soviet state and described their implications in the areas of social security and medicine. In this chapter I will try to summarize the main characteristics of those forces and briefly present possible alternatives to the present nature of both the Soviet state and Soviet medicine.

As stated in the introduction as well as elsewhere in this volume, the method of historical analysis that I have followed is the one of historical materialism, which sees change as the result of the interaction between objective forces (i.e., the material conditions of the Soviet Union in the different periods described in the previous chapters) and subjective forces, including the prevalent ideology of the dominant group (i.e., the Communist Party in the case of the Soviet Union).

In the analysis of the subjective forces, the ideas of Lenin, the founder of the Soviet Union, are of paramount importance. And a detailed analysis of Lenin's writings clearly shows that, contrary to what official Soviet (and Chinese) theoreticians sometimes seem to believe, Lenin was not an absolutely consistent and infallible individual, nor was he, as Carlo has clearly shown, the guardian angel of the revolution.[1] Lenin's views varied quite substantially with time. And within his continuously changing perception, Lenin was far from always consistent. Let me hasten to add that these remarks on Lenin's changing thought should not be perceived as in any way minimizing the great role—a fundamental one—that Lenin played in the history of the socialist movement. Indeed, these comments are made with the intention of depicting not a superhuman Lenin but rather an earthy, fallible, and, I may add, more attractive one. Due to the importance that the different changes in Lenin's thought had on the development of the Soviet state, let me briefly summarize them.

Changes in the Leninist Strategy for Change

The first analysis of revolutionary strategy was written by Lenin, in 1895, in his *Draft Program of the Social Democratic Party*. In this work, he believed that the workers' struggles at the working place (struggles aimed at obtaining better economic and working conditions) would automatically lead to their struggle against the entire social order which was based on the exploitation of labor by capital. The general strikes of 1895–1896, however, had quite an effect on Lenin and led him to modify his views. Indeed, those great strikes ended without any significant political accomplishments; they were not followed by a demand for change in the social order. Rather, the only tangible result of the strikes was the very limited social legislation discussed in Chapter 1. This led Lenin to believe that the working class by itself could only become involved in and could only make economic but not political demands. Thus, he felt the need for a political party composed of a small vanguard—the majority of them intellectuals of petit bourgeois class backgrounds—which would politically educate and lead the working class in the revolutionary struggle. Indeed, in his famous *What Is To Be Done?* (mistakenly assumed to be Lenin's definitive work on revolution), Lenin wrote that "class political consciousness can be brought to the workers only from *without,* that is, only from outside the economic struggle, from outside the sphere of relations between workers and employers"[2] and he postulated that class consciousness would be brought to the workers by "educated representatives of the majority classes." This group would be a cadre of highly-disciplined individuals who, because of the clandestine and paramilitary conditions under which they would be required to operate, would need a hierarchical and centralized line of command. This group became the Bolshevik Party; it would politicize the working class and help it translate its economic demands into political ones. In summary, it would be the historical role of the Party to lead the socialist revolution and thus to liberate the working class. The task of the Party was to lead and that of the working class was to follow.

The first October Revolution, of 1905, which happened just after Lenin had written *What Is To Be Done?,* had a profound impact on Lenin and forced him to again change his thought. Indeed, that revolution took place without any Party participation, much less leadership. The workers took over the factories spontaneously—via the factory committees—and established the Soviets, the councils whose members were elected directly by the workers, peasants, and soldiers. As Lenin had indicated, the first October Revolution caught the revolutionary parties completely unprepared and by surprise. Stimulated by those events, Lenin wrote, just after the repressed October Revolution of 1905, his well-known *Two Tactics,* in which he indicated that "we—the Bolsheviks—rely fully and solely on the *free initiative* of the working masses themselves."[3] According to this new work, the working class was the leader and the Party was the assistant and follower. Quite a change from his thesis outlined in *What Is To Be Done?*

It is important to underline that despite this substantial change, the second and finally successful October Revolution, of 1917, still caught the Bolshevik Party unprepared and by surprise. Lenin, however, responded by fully supporting the spontaneous creation of the Soviets by the working class and by his famous call for "All power to the Soviets," reiterating the fundamental revolutionary importance of the Soviets produced by the creativity of the masses. And in his work, *State and Revolution,* written in 1917, he spoke of the working class and not of the Party as the governing force of the Soviets! It is in this work that Lenin established the definition of socialism as being the only political system that is based on the massive and direct participation of the masses in the direction of the state. And that participation would take place via the Soviets, the organs of government controlled *by* the workers and not just *for* the workers (however well-intentioned the vanguard party may have been when governing *for* the workers). This direct form of government was supposed to be guaranteed by the Soviets being elected directly by the workers, peasants, and soldiers, by their having executive in addition to legislative powers, and by their having elected members who would be continuously subject to recall by the electorate. Moreover, the forces of production were supposed to actively participate in the running of the institutions under the direction of the Soviets.

Comparing that idea of socialism, as reflected in Lenin's *State and Revolution,* with the actual socialism practiced in today's Soviet Union may be similar, as Colletti indicates, to comparing the initial outline presented in the Sermon on the Mount with the reality of the Vatican.[4] Why the disparity? Let me state that, as indicated before, no doubt the easiest explanation for that situation is the one most frequently given by conservative and liberal authors alike, i.e., the all-pervasive human condition and the inevitable and unavoidable sclerosis of any political system. Disagreeing with this profoundly conservative interpretation of history, I have in this volume presented an alternative one, indicating that Leninist ideology had to be molded and adapted to the specific objective conditions of the Soviet Union at that time—its material base. The awareness of this relationship does not mean (as economic determinists would postulate) that those material conditions of the early Soviet Union determined the nature of the Leninist ideology. Rather, that ideology had to be implemented within specific historical circumstances—material and otherwise—which characterized the Soviet Union of that time. Indeed, as Marx indicated: "Men make their own history, but they do not make it just as they please; they do not make it under circumstances chosen by themselves, but under circumstances directly encountered, given, and transmitted from the past."[5] It could not have been said better.

Why the Centralization of the Soviet State?

According to Lenin's *State and Revolution,* the political objective of the revolution was the increased control of the government by the Soviets, as was explained in Chapter 2. There would be local, regional, republic, and national Soviets elected directly by the majority of the population (excepting members of the aristocracy, the property-owning classes, priests, and imbeciles), with an increased decentralization of power leading to direct control and governance of the institutions by the collectivity of producers.

In the War Communism period, and as explained in Chapter 3, experience with the implementation of this governing model was, according to Lenin, far from successful. The Soviets in the rural areas were, to a large degree, practically controlled by the petite bourgeoisie due to the low degree of politicization of the peasantry. And in the urban areas, the working class, the progressive force behind the October Revolution, was practically decimated. The October Revolution of 1917 was thus rapidly losing its constituency. This new situation strengthened the awareness in Lenin that socialism (and even less, instant socialism) was not possible in a poor country. Prior to the implementation of socialism, there was a need to develop the country, i.e., to develop the material basis of the economy so as to allow for a later implementation of socialist democracy. In Marxist terms, the development of the forces of production was a prerequisite for the change in the social relations of production. The Soviet Union had to be massively industrialized, following the lines analyzed and described in Chapter 4; and the Party had to provide the active leadership for that process of industrialization. Consequently the Soviets, as well as the unions or any other organizations, changed their governing function and became the implementers of Party policy. According to Lenin, the trade unions (and the Soviets) had to collaborate closely and constantly with "the government in all political and economic activities which are guided by the class conscious vanguard of the working class—the Communist Party."[6] The Lenin of *What Is To Be Done?* took over the Lenin of *State and Revolution.* In this scheme of things, the Party was supposed to direct and lead the process of industrialization in the Soviet Union. And for that purpose it needed (1) the utilization and further strengthening of the inherited Czarist state, and (2) the dependency of all political institutions— Soviets, unions, and everything else—on the Party. Thus were the possibilities for the future appearance of a Stalin established.

In this situation, then, the primary priority was the development of the forces of production. And for that, the political leadership chose the only model of material development known at that time, the Western European model, i.e., massive investment in heavy industrial production. Instead of industrialization by private enterprise, however, as in the capitalist world, the Soviet Union was going to do it under the direction of the Party, under the administration of the modified but inherited Czarist state machinery, and with the assistance of the newly created technocracy. Three basic groups were then established in the direction of Soviet industrialization: the party, the bureaucracy, and the technocracy, with a gradient of authority from the first to the last.

As was described in Chapter 4, that process of Soviet industrialization, which in its major characteristics still continues today, was typified by:

1. *a priority given to heavy industry,* with the production of nonconsumer goods to a degree that today, sixty years after the October Revolution, the Soviet Union continues to stress heavy industry at the expense of consumer goods and social services;
2. *an agriculture which is supposed to serve industry,* while industry is not primarily agriculture-oriented, e.g., toward the production of agricultural machinery, but toward heavy industry;
3. *a vertical hierarchicalization of responsibility and authority, with increased specialization and division of labor* which establish a line of command that originates
   a. from the top echelons of the Party to the bureaucrat;
   b. from the bureaucrat to the technocrat;
   c. from the workers who work mentally to those working manually;
   d. from the urban authority to the rural ones; and
4. *reliance on individual and material incentives for the attainment of productivity goals,* and the reliance on social management for finding the solution to social problems.

Why this Evolution of the Soviet Experience?

As indicated in Chapter 4, this evolution of industrialization was very much the result of (1) the commitment of the Party to develop the forces of production as a primary condition for the development, in a subsequent stage, of socialism, and (2) the understanding of development in the same terms that prevailed in the capitalist industrialized societies. The strategy then was to industrialize following the same type of industrialization found in the Western world, not under the direction of the bourgeoisie but of a working-class-based party. And at issue was not changing the nature of the socialist state and the socialist society, but rather using the already existent state to direct the process of industrialization as copied and imported from the Western world. In this model—the Kautskyan and Stalinist model—the state was not to change (as the Lenin of *State and Revolution* wanted), but rather it was supposed to be used by a minority, supposedly representative of the working class, for its own purposes, i.e., the industrialization of the USSR.

This strategy that makes the development of the material basis of the economy the primary condition for a later implementation of socialism (a later development that never seems to come) is what Bettelheim calls economism,[7] and it is reflected in the belief that (1) the public ownership of the means of production is synonymous with the socialist transformation of the relations of production; (2) the socialist relations of production, i.e., socialism, have to wait until the country has reached a certain level of economic development; (3) the state (after the abolition of private ownership and the disappearance of the capitalists as the dominant class) reflects the interests of the working class; and (4) the function of the state is primarily to better manage the economy. Within this set of beliefs, social and political issues are reduced to managerial ones. And the solution to either social or political problems is to have more and better social management by the state. Let me add here that today this state managerialism is increasingly applauded by Western conservative and liberal authors alike as a sign of the maturity of the Soviet system, and as a sign of its having transcended the cumbersome and irrelevant ideologies which have now been relegated to a place of mere historical interest for ideologues. Meanwhile, those authors conclude that "their system looks more and more like ours." And this means, of course, that it looks better.

What Is the Alternative? Brief Notes on Socialism

The alternative to the economism summarized above is to interpret the concept of the development of the forces of production in a far more fundamental way than the one previously described and held by the past and present leadership of the Soviet Union. Indeed, the development of the forces of production has to be seen not only in economic but also in social and political terms. In other words, it cannot be seen as the development of material wealth, technology, machines, and capital, but must be seen primarily in terms of the human agents of production. To accept, as Stalinists do, the sequential route of socialist development in which the growth of material wealth or capital accumulation precedes socialist development—the growth of socialist cooperative and democratic relations—is to replicate the capitalist concept of development which assumes the primacy of capital accumulation in the system. Indeed, there is a need in a socialist society for making the economy's development subject to and dependent on a higher priority—the development of a new political and social consciousness in the individual, and of a cooperative and democratic society. To do otherwise, as Che Guevara used to say, is "to assume that the task of building socialism in a backward society is for the revolutionary leaders to correct the historical mistake of coming into power prematurely and force capitalistic relations into one's own country."[8]

Let me underline here that what I am espousing is not, of course, antigrowth or the "back-to-nature" movement which is prevalent among some sectors of the maverick U.S. radical movement, but rather the conditioning of that growth to the most primordial task of developing socialist, cooperative, and democratic relations of production. The latter has to precede the former and not vice versa. As Fidel Castro once said: "The issue is not creating political awareness with wealth but rather creating wealth with political awareness."[9] Thus, socialist development requires giving priority to:

1. a massive participation of the population not only in the implementation but also in the decision-making process of collective activities. The active involvement of mass organizations is needed in the direction and implementation of the policies of production, composition, and distribution of the national product. In fact, this is the meaning of increased reliance on the masses in the direction of the state, with political consciousness, mass participation, and industrial and institutional democracy being important components of that process; and

2. a change in the ideological construct of society, with a redefinition of the pattern of social relations and the organs of legitimization (education and medicine, among others). This redefinition should determine a change from the reliance of hierarchical authority and discipline toward the reliance on cooperative effort and collective support.

Needless to say, that socialist development will not take place automatically, but rather will go through an evolutionary process which takes the time of generations. In the evaluation of a socialist society's experience, however, what is important is the direction of change, whether *toward or away from* those objectives. And this change should be aimed, in its last stage, at the creation of a "commonwealth in which human beings would find harmony among themselves and with their environment." It is, in brief, the process of going from one type of society to another, from one type of power to another, and last but not least, from one type of medicine to another.

The Nature of Medicine and the Health Sector in the Soviet Union

As was indicated and shown in the different chapters of this volume, the nature of Soviet medicine and its health services (and also of social security) was very much the result of the dialectical interaction between the objective conditions (the material basis of the USSR) and the subjective ones (the ideology of the leadership of the Communist Party). And as was also indicated, both the meaning and nature of medicine, as well as the functions and structure of the health sector (and social security), were very much the result of the Communist Party leadership's commitment to the massive industrialization of the Soviet Union. As part of that commitment, the primary purpose of medicine (and of social security) was to contribute to the development of the forces of production, understanding the development of those forces in the previously-defined sense of the growth of the material basis of the Soviet economy.

It is interesting to note here that reflecting that commitment to industrialization, we found (in Chapters 4-8) that the evolution of medicine and the health services in the Soviet Union followed a process similar to the evolution of the industrial model. Indeed, in the same way that the model of industrialization that developed in the USSR was similar to the model of industrialization prevalent in capitalist Europe, the model of medicine that developed in the USSR—an imported one—was also similar to the model of medicine prevalent in capitalist Europe at that time, i.e., scientific medicine. In that respect, we see in medicine a development similar to what we saw in the development of industrialization. In other words, the Communist Party's leadership did not change either the model of the state or the model of industrialization, but rather used both for its own purpose to develop the material basis of the USSR. Similarly, that leadership did not change the nature of scientific medicine, but rather used the prevalent model of medicine existent at that time for its own purpose. In summary, the primary characteristic of that process was the change of control over the instruments, namely, the state mechanism, industrialization, and medicine, from one group—the nobility—to another—the political party. But there was no change of the instruments themselves.

Let me underline here that that change of control over those instruments has no doubt meant considerable, meaningful, and beneficial quantitative changes in the production and distribution of resources both within and outside the health sector, as described in detail in this volume. But, as also shown, these changes have not affected the nature of the instruments themselves, i.e., the concept of medicine has not evolved from one in which the individual is a passive recipient and consumer of services—as in bourgeois medicine—to one where the individual sees that the betterment of his health is closely linked to the betterment of the collectivity and in which the collectivity of newly-conscious individuals decides and produces the conditions for both collective and individual health.

The Evolution of Soviet Medicine

The political commitment of the Communist leadership to the centralized direction of the process of industrialization also determined the further application of the model of industrialization to medicine. As was shown in Chapters 6-8, we find today:

1. a political and managerial centralization of the medical care system;
2. a division of labor in medicine with (a) medicine divided into branches (preventive medicine, adult medicine, and maternal and child medicine) and specialties; and (b) a hierarchicalization of labor within the labor force in the health sector (as was shown in Chapter 7);
3. a division of responsibilities in which the "expert" is the active actor and the patients and potential patients, i.e., the collectivity, are the passive ones; and

4. an increased centralization of resources in hospitals, specialized care, and the urban areas (as was shown in Chapters 6 and 8).

Parallel to these characteristics, we also find a depoliticization of the medical care system and a strengthening of the managerial elements within the system. And in this scheme of things, the political leadership of the Party perceived that the main problems of the system required managerial and not political solutions. As reported in Chapter 8, the declarations of the leaders of Soviet medicine are very similar indeed to the declarations of our own leaders of medicine in capitalist societies. Their responses to the uneven distribution of resources, the high costs of medical care, and medical problems (e.g., alcoholism) are to improve and strengthen the management of the medical care system and increase the number of resources. Needless to say, this depoliticization of the system is (as was shown in Chapter 8) applauded by the leaders of our own medical care system as a sign of both maturity and of having transcended ideologies (the concern of incorrigible ideologues), and also as a sign of an increased convergence of both systems. Actually, one logical step in this sharing of managerial ideologies has been the creation in Vienna of an International Institute of Operations Research and Management Sciences whose efforts are aimed at the use of management skills and tools in the solutions to social problems and which is jointly sponsored by both the USSR and the U.S. governments. The objective of the institute is to learn "how to solve the ardent social problems that occur in our countries, and assist other countries in the resolution of those problems." In summary, managerialism is viewed as the solution to the problems in our medical care system.

Alternatives to the Managerialism of Soviet Medicine

Repeating what others have eloquently said, I have indicated that the only alternative to that managerial approach of society is the democratization and politicization of the system. Similarly, we find that the only alternative to the managerialism of medicine is its democratization and politicization. In order to explain the meaning of those terms, we have to return to the writings of Marx and Engels. And the most immediate impression that a reading of their works conveys is that socialism is certainly not a managerial theory but a political one. In other words, socialism is primarily the political process whereby the differences between rural and urban strata, mental and manual work, governors and the governed, and experts and laymen are supposed to start disappearing. This applies to medicine as well as to any other sector.

And as I indicated previously, a primary motive that must exist for that socialization to take place is the massive and direct involvement of the population in its affairs—political, economic, and social. As the Lenin of *State and*

Revolution pointed out, socialism is self-government of the population. What are the operational implications of this abstract proposition for medicine? Many. Let me list the ones I consider most important.

First, priority must be given to the development of socialist social relations. Among other things, this means that at any stage of development a socialist society has to have human liberation and not capital accumulation as the primary purpose of its development. And that human development takes place not by putting the politicians (the "experts" in politicking), the party members, or the technical experts in command of institutions, but rather by having the massive and direct involvement of the population in the running of their political, economic, and social institutions; in other words, the increased takeover by the governed of the governors' functions. In the health sector, this means the control of the health institutions by the citizens of the communities served by those institutions and by the workers in those institutions, i.e., the widespread involvement of the mass organizations not only in the implementation but also in the generation of health policies. Actually, the massive mobilization of the Cuban population in education and health campaigns determined a conscious politicization of the majority of citizens involved in those campaigns. And a similar experience is being reported on the post-Cultural Revolution in China. It is worth underlining that mass participation should (1) be a continuous and not a sporadic event, and (2) take place not only in the implementation but equally, or even more importantly, in the political generation of those programs.

Second, there must be a dilution of the division of labor in medicine, with the declassization, democratization, and deprofessionalization of medicine. Let me add here that I am aware, of course, of the prevalent argument in our societies that because of the massive development of technology, our technological and industrialized societies require an unavoidable centralization of their direction, with an unfortunate but inevitable increase in social distance between the governors and the governed, the experts and the laymen, and the skilled and unskilled. Actually, this argument of the need for centralization, supposedly due to the industrialization of our societies, is also heard in medicine where the centralization of its decision-making is seen as the unavoidable result of its increased technologization.

As I have indicated elsewhere,[10] this thesis assumes that industrialization causes the centralization of power. But quite to the contrary, historical evidence shows that the centralization of power caused the process and type of industrialization that works primarily for the benefit of the governors and not of the governed. The real cause of our undemocratic systems, both in the USSR and the United States, is not the complexity of the mode of production or the process of industrialization, but rather the frightening centralization of political and economic power in both societies that causes that type of development. And this is, incidentally, quite clear in medicine as well. Indeed, the technological component of medicine, although large in budget, is small in terms of effect. And, as quite a number of authors have proven, most of medicine does not require much technology. Despite this, the technological argument is continuously used as a justification for the highly centralized direction of medicine. Here again, we find that the primary cause for the centralization and technologization of medicine is the concentration of political and administrative power that determines that centralized and technological development. The only solution to that technologization of medicine is its democratization and massive politicization, which would lead to its deprofessionalization.

In summary, and evolving from the presentation in this volume, it seems that in any socialist society (and as I have shown in another volume,[11] also in any capitalist society) there are two basic forces in the health sector that interact dialectically, with the predominance of one over the other determining not only the distribution of resources but also the understanding of medicine. Indeed, on the one hand, we have what we may call, for lack of better words, the *centripetal* forces, of which the most important one, the determinant one, is the force toward the political centralization of power by the dominant groups and/or class. That political centralization of power enables and facilitates the appearance of the other centripetal forces of specialization, professionalization, urbanization, and the hospital orientation of medicine. Moreover, centralization of political power also strengthens the individual and not the collective responsibility for medicine. Indeed, medicine is considered the responsibility of the professional politician and the expert. And that distribution of responsibility puts the citizen in a passive role, i.e., a subject to be acted upon.

And acting in the opposite direction, we find the *centrifugal* forces that are primarily determined by the democratization and decentralization of the system which enable and facilitate the appearance of other centrifugal forces such as deprofessionalization, despecialization, and an emphasis on rural areas and on community and ambulatory care. That democratization and politicization of medicine ultimately lead to a redefinition of not only the practice of medicine (including priorities in the health sector) but, most importantly, of the content of medicine in which medicine is increasingly perceived as a collective and not just an individual responsibility, and where the differences between the expert and the layman, the governor and the governed, and the urban and rural content and practice of medicine start disappearing.

Empirical Evidence of the Dialectical Interplay of Centrifugal Vis-à-Vis Centripetal Forces in Medicine

Needless to say, that dialectical model, as any other theoretical model, needs to be tested by empirical methods for its legitimation. But the experiences of Chile and Cuba that I am familiar with, and reports on the post-Cultural Revolution in

China, seem to provide, if not conclusive, then at least supportive evidence of the model described above. Indeed, the experience in the health sector of Allende's Chile, where the communities and the workers increasingly took over the running of the health institutions, shows how the citizens' control over those institutions also meant the strengthening of centrifugal forces such as the increased deprofessionalization of the delivery of health care, a greater emphasis on community and social medicine, and the redefinition of the nature and meaning of medicine and its priorities.[12] The subsequent and tragic fascist coup recentralized the political direction, emphasizing the centripetal forces of professionalization, hospitalization, and urbanization.

Similarly, an analysis of the health sector in Cuba clearly shows the existence of those two forces. The forces that act in favor of centralization, hierarchicalization, hospitalization, professionalization, and urbanization increasingly conflict with those forces that demand decentralization with emphasis on democratization and politicization, rural medicine, ambulatory care, and deprofessionalization. Specifically, a conflict appears between some elements of the political leadership who, in alliance with the leaders of academic medicine (trained for the most part in terms of scientific medicine and who want to improve the standards of "excellence" of Cuban medicine), push for a central direction of social policy and the new democratic forces that demand a continuous and profound reappraisal of hospital-oriented medicine and a change of direction for medicine which would emphasize deprofessionalization, democratization, the establishment of health centers, and ambulatory and rural care.

Similarly, in China (until the Cultural Revolution) the centripetal forces forced Mao to define the Ministry of Health of the People's Republic of China as the Ministry of Urban Lords. To the degree that, during and after the Cultural Revolution, the trend toward political centralization seems to have been reversed in that country, there has been a strengthening of the centrifugal forces over the centripetal ones.

Conclusion: Nationalization Is Not Socialization

To the founders of socialism, then, it was clear that socialism was the political process toward direct government by the people over the political, economic, and social resources (including health) that they produced. To quote once again from Lenin's *State and Revolution*, "Socialism is the process towards the self-government of the masses." In that respect, the takeover of the state by a minority group which represents the working class is a socialist step only when it is part of a process that will change the nature of that state toward extending its power to the majority and not to the minority of the population. As Lenin also stated, to limit socialism to the takeover of the state by a party, which was what Kautsky advocated and Stalin practiced, would be simply "to substitute one group of masters by another one."

In the same vein and for the same reason, the nationalization of a sector of economic or social activity (like the health sector) can only be referred to as the socialization of that activity when it improves the direct control over that activity by the population. In other words, nationalization is socialization only when it is part of a process toward the democratization and self-government of the people. And the degree of socialization in that activity can be measured by the degree of popular participation in the running of that activity.

Contrary to that definition, we can see that the word socialism is frequently used as if it were identical to nationalization. But there is a continuous need to make the aforementioned distinction between the two. The lack of that distinction creates a continuous obfuscation that none other than Engels clearly warned against.

. . . since Bismarck adopted state ownership a certain spurious socialism has made its appearance here and there, even degenerating into a kind of flunkeyism —which declares that *all* taking over by the state, even of the Bismarckian kind, is in itself socialistic. If, however, the taking over of the tobacco trade by the State was socialistic, Napoleon and Metternich would rank among the founders of socialism. If the Belgian state, for quite ordinary political and financial reasons, constructed its own main railway lines; if Bismarck . . . took over the main railway lines in Prussia, simply in order to be better able to organize and use them for war, to train the railway officials as the government's voting cattle, and especially to secure a new source of revenue independent of parliamentary votes,—such actions were in no sense socialist measures. Otherwise the Royal Maritime Company, the Royal Porcelain Manufacture, and even the regimental tailors in the army, would be socialist institutions.[13]

As Walter Kendall has indicated:

Indeed, following the tradition of Engels, one might point out that if all that was required for socialism was the ownership of property by a collective organism and the administration of that property by a self-reproducing oligarchical elite, then the Catholic Church has been a socialist institution for twenty centuries. If all that is required for socialism is production according to a plan, for use and not for profit, under the supervision of an authoritarian command structure, then the prison workshop is the proper prototype of a socialist community.[14]

Indeed, nationalization has frequently been advocated and supported by sectors of the capitalist class to strengthen rather than weaken the prevalent set of power relations in our capitalist system. Coates has convincingly shown how many nationalization measures taken under both the Labour and Conservative Parties in Great Britain have reinforced control by the dominant class over the high points of the British economy.[15]

In summary, then, nationalization may or may not be socialization. It depends on who controls it and, most importantly, for what purpose. And the same holds true in the health sector. Let me underline here that nothing I have said should be interpreted as being against the nationalization of the health sector or any other sector for that matter. Rather, nationalization, which in itself may have been a political improvement over the past situation, has to be part and parcel of a broader policy for the democratization of the health sector in order to be defined as socialization. Indeed, the nationalization of the health sector in Great Britain in 1948 by the Labour Government was a very positive step that undoubtedly benefited the majority of the British population. And the creation of the nationalized and state-run health services has been a positive development over the previous historical stage of national health insurance. But, as Draper and Smart have clearly indicated, the NHS and its institutions have not received any direct form of input from the British population. And the reforms that are currently taking place in the NHS are primarily aimed at even further strengthening the managerial forces as opposed to strengthening the workers' and communities' input.[16] Based on this, I would conclude that the NHS—as well as today's Soviet health sector—is a nationalized but not a socialized health sector. Indeed, I would define the NHS or the Soviet health sector as socialized sectors only if they had developed an institutional framework that would not only have allowed but also stimulated the popular involvement, participation, and direct control of the institutions of the sector by the communities served by those institutions and by the workers of those institutions.

Let me end by clarifying that I do not believe that socialization is just nationalization plus workers' and community control. Indeed, I believe that in order to have meaningful and continuous mass participation in the running of the institutions, there is a need for the continuous politicization of the majority of the population, aimed at transforming it from a passive to an active agent of its history. And this applies to medicine as well. In other words, the process of institutional and industrial democracy cannot be seen as a mechanical and independent process, but rather as part and parcel of a larger process for the overall democratization of that society. Similarly, socialization of medicine is not just the nationalization of medicine and the democratization of its institutions, but, more importantly, the massive transformation of the population from being passive recipients to active agents in the redefinition of health, medicine, and its institutions—a transformation that takes place as part and parcel of their becoming the agents and not the subjects of history.

Appendix
Physician-Population Ratios and
Percentage of Urban Population
by Soviet Oblast, 1959 and 1971

	Physician Population Ratio (per 10,000 population)		Percent of Urban Population	
	1959	*1971*	*1959*	*1971*
Northwest Region				
Arkhangelskaya oblast	15.4	26.2	52	68
Vologodskaya oblast	9.4	19.7	35	50
Leningradskaya oblast	45.3			
Leningrad	55.5	71.5	100	
Murmanskaya oblast	29.5	42.2	92	88
Novgorodnaya oblast	12.0	21.9	38	56
Pskovskaya oblast	11.1	22.3	27	46
Karelskaya oblast	15.9	29.1	63	71
Komi ASSR	14.8	28.4	59	64
Central Region				
Bryanskaya oblast	9.2	17.4	35	50
Vladimirskaya oblast	11.8	22.8	57	69
Ivanovskaya oblast	19.2	31.4	66	77
Kalininskaya oblast	12.1	24.4	44	60
Kalugskaya oblast	10.8	22.9	37	54
Kostromskaya oblast	10.1	20.7	39	58
Moscow	62.5	76.7	100	100
Moskovskaya oblast	39.2	31.7		
Orlovskaya oblast	8.2	18.9	24	43
Ryazanskaya oblast	11.7	26.7	30	50
Smolenskaya oblast	14.6	28.2	32	51
Tulskaya oblast	11.7	22.1	61	74
Yaroslavnaya oblast	16.6	31.4	58	72
Volga Vyatskii Region				
Gorkovskaya oblast	16.2	28.9	52	66
Kirovskaya oblast	9.3	20.0	37	58
Mariskaya ASSR	10.2	21.0	28	43
Mordovskaya ASSR	7.7	17.6	18	38
Chuvashkaya ASSR	8.3	17.1	24	38
Central Chernozemnye Region				
Belogorskaya oblast	7.3	18.7	18	39
Voronezhskaya oblast	15.1	26.9	35	48
Kurskaya oblast	10.3	20.6	20	36
Lipetskayà oblast	10.3	19.4	30	47
Tambovskaya oblast	10.1	16.6	26	42
Pavolskii Region				
Astratrakhanskaya oblast	29.4	42.0	52	62
Kuybyshevskaya oblast	22.4	32.0	62	74

119

	Physician Population Ratio (per 10,000 population)		Percent of Urban Population	
	1959	1971	1959	1971
Penzenskaya oblast	9.9	16.6	33	47
Sarotovskaya oblast	23.7	33.5	54	67
Ulyanovskaya oblast	10.2	20.6	36	55
Bashkirskaya ASSR	11.0	19.2	38	50
Kalmetskaya ASSR	9.9	22.2	21	37
Tatarskaya ASSR	16.9	23.5	42	54
Northern Caucasus Region				
Krasnodarskii Kray	17.2	28.8	50	64
Stavropolskii Kray	20.5	31.1	30	45
Rostovskaya oblast	19.0	27.9	57	65
Dagestanskaya ASSR	13.4	21.2	30	36
Kabardino-Bulgarian ASSR	14.7	27.3	38	53
North Assetian ASSR	28.8	43.5	53	66
Chechen-Ingush ASSR	14.9	18.7	41	42
Urals Region				
Kurganskaya oblast	8.9	17.7	33	46
Orenburgskaya oblast	12.7	21.3	45	55
Permskaya oblast	15.6	22.8	59	69
Sverdlovskaya oblast	17.7	26.0	76	82
Chelyabinskaya oblast	16.1	24.3	.76	79
Udmurtskaya ASSR	14.6	26.5	44	60
West Siberian Region				
Altaiskii Kray	8.9	19.2	33	48
Kemerovskaya oblast	13.8	25.0	77	83
Novosibirskaya oblast	17.6	30.0	55	67
Omskaya oblast	20.0	30.9	43	58
Tomskaya oblast	21.2	31.0	47	61
Tumenskaya oblast	11.4	23.2	32	52
South Siberian Region				
Krasnoyarskii Dray	14.0	23.2	50	64
Irkootskaya oblast	18.8	25.3	62	74
Chitinskaya oblast	15.3	23.4	55	59
Tuvinskaya ASSR	13.8	23.9	29	39
Far Eastern Region				
Primorskii Kray	18.4	28.2	67	74
Chabarovskii Kray	23.6	33.0	74	79
Amvrskaya oblast	16.2	25.3	60	63
Kamchatskaya oblast	31.5	44.0	64	78
Magadanskaya oblast	39.3	49.9	89	74
Sachalinskaya oblast	22.8	37.5	75	81
Yakutskaya ASSR	20.6	24.2	49	58
Kalingradskaya oblast	24.7	34.6	64	74

Sources: *Zdravookhranenie v SSSR, 1960: Statisticheskii Sbornik* (Moscow: Gosstatizdat, 1960); and *Narodnoe Khaziaistvo v RSFSR*, 1972: Statisticheskoe Sbornik (Moscow: Statistika, 1972).

Notes

Notes

Introduction

1. Henry Sigerist, *Medicine and Health in the Soviet Union* (New York: The Citadel Press, 1947).

2. Harry Braverman, "The Successes, the Failures, and the Prospects," in Leo Huberman et al., *Fifty Years of Soviet Power* (New York: Monthly Review Press, 1967), p. 23.

3. Lucio Colletti, *From Rousseau to Lenin: Studies in Ideology and Society* (New York: Monthly Review Press, 1972), p. 226.

4. Vicente Navarro, "Social Policy Issues: An Explanation of the Composition, Nature and Functions of the Present Health Sector of the United States," *Bulletin of the New York Academy of Medicine,* 51, 1 (1975):199-234.

5. C. Wright Mills, *The Sociological Imagination* (New York: Grove Press, 1959).

6. Norman Birnbaum, *Toward a Critical Sociology* (New York: Oxford University Press, 1971).

7. H. A. Ronaghy and S. Solter, "Is the Chinese Barefoot Doctor Exportable to Rural Iran?" *Lancet,* 1, 7870 (1974):1331-1333.

Chapter 1
Pre-Soviet Russia

1. Alexander Gerschenkron, "The Rate of Growth in Russia," *Journal of Economic History,* 7, supplement (1947):146 and 155.

2. David Lane, *Politics and Society in the USSR* (New York: Random House, 1970), p. 25.

3. Ibid., p. 29.

4. P. I. Lyashchenko, *History of the National Economy of Russia* (New York: Macmillan, 1949), p. 382.

5. A. G. Rashin, *Formirovanie Rabochego Klassa Rossii* (Moscow, 1958), p. 48.

6. Warren W. Eason, "Population Changes," in Cyril E. Black (ed.), *The Transformation of Russian Society* (Cambridge, Mass.: Harvard University Press, 1960), p. 83. It should be noted, however, that the overall rate of urbanization in Russia was lower than in most Western countries. Similar figures for the percentage of the population living in urban areas in 1913 were: Great Britain, 50 percent; United States, 33 percent; Germany, 54 percent; and

England, 77 percent. See Karl-Heinz Ruffman, "Social Change in Russia Prior to the October Revolution," in Boris Meissner (ed.), *Social Change in the Soviet Union* (Notre Dame, Ind.: Notre Dame Press, 1972), p. 19.

7. For a further discussion of land ownership in pre-Soviet Russia, see Ruffman, "Social Change in Russia Prior to the October Revolution," p. 10.

8. Theodore H. Von Lave, *Sergei Witte and the Industrialization of Russia* (New York: The Citadel Press, 1943), p. 26.

9. For a brief review of mortality and morbidity in pre-Soviet Russia, see Sigerist, *Medicine and Health in the Soviet Union,* pp. 3-21, and Gordon Hyde, *The Soviet Health Service: A Historical and Comparative Study* (London: Lawrence and Wishart, 1974), p. 13.

10. For a description of Zemstvo government, see Alexander Vucinich, "The State and the Local Community," in Black, *Transformation of Russian Society.*

11. Sigerist, *Medicine and Health in the Soviet Union,* p. 10.

12. Quoted in Lane, *Politics and Society in the USSR,* p. 32.

13. Ruffman, "Social Change in Russia Prior to the October Revolution," p. 19.

14. Charles Bettelheim, *Class Struggles in the USSR. First Period: 1917–1923* (New York: Monthly Review Press, 1976), p. 158.

15. Eason, "Population Changes," p. 88.

16. For a detailed description of the composition and functions of the Duma, see G. A. Hosking, *The Russian Constitutional Experiment: Government and Duma 1907–1914* (London: Cambridge University Press, 1973).

17. For an in-depth analysis of the political formations in pre-Soviet Russia, see E. H. Carr, *The Bolshevik Revolution, 1917–1923,* Vol. 1 (Middlesex: Penguin Books, 1969).

18. For an account of social security in pre-Soviet Russia, see Gaston V. Rimlinger, *Welfare Policy and Industrialization in Europe, America, and Russia* (New York: John Wiley & Sons, 1971), p. 245. See also Bernice Madison, "The Organization of Welfare Services," in Black, *Transformation of Russian Society,* p. 518.

19. Madison, "Organization of Welfare Services," p. 521.

20. Carr, *Bolshevik Revolution,* Vol. I, p. 64.

21. V. I. Lenin, *Collected Works,* Vol. XVII (Moscow: Foreign Languages Publishing House, 1963), p. 476.

22. Ibid., pp. 478–479.

23. See, for example, André Gorz, *Socialism and Revolution* (New York: Anchor Books, 1973) and *Strategy for Labor: A Radical Proposal* (Boston: Beacon Press, 1964).

24. Sigerist, *Medicine and Health in the Soviet Union*, p. 15.

25. There is not yet a comprehensive reference on the historical development of feldsherism in Russia.

26. For an example representative of this viewpoint, see the report by Dr. Nikolai Ekk, published in 1885 in *Mezhdunarodnaia Klinika* and quoted in Mark Field, *Soviet Specialized Medicine* (New York: The Free Press, 1967), p. 24.

27. Both Sigerist and Field emphasize this possible reason for Zemstvo medicine. See also, N. M. Frieden, "Physicians in Pre-Revolutionary Russia: Professionals or Servants of the State?" *Bulletin of the History of Medicine* 49, 1 (1975):20-29.

28. Hyde, *Soviet Health Service*, p. 13.

29. Quoted in Field, *Soviet Specialized Medicine*, p. 21.

30. Sigerist, *Medicine and Health in the Soviet Union*, p. 8.

31. Thomas McKeown, "A Historical Appraisal of the Medical Task," in Gordon McLachlan and McKeown (eds.), *Medical History and Medical Care* (London: Oxford University Press, 1971), pp. 29-57.

32. Ibid., p. 29.

33. Hyde, *Soviet Health Service*, p. 21.

34. Sigerist, *Medicine and Health in the Soviet Union*, p. 13.

35. Frieden, "Physicians in Pre-Revolutionary Russia," p. 25.

36. National Academy of Sciences (USSR), *Historical Bulletin* 20, 6 (1951):32. (In Russian)

37. Ibid., p. 12.

38. Colletti, *From Rousseau to Lenin.*

39. Karl Marx, "The German Ideology," in *Selected Works*, Vol. 1 (London: Lawrence and Wishart, 1962), p. 47.

40. Frederick Engels, "Letter to J. Bloch, 21 September 1890," in Marx and Engels, *Selected Correspondence* (Moscow, 1963), p. 498.

Chapter 2
The Soviet Revolution and War Communism: 1917-1921

1. For a detailed account of the events surrounding the February Revolution, see Carr, *Bolshevik Revolution*, Vol. 1, p. 81 ff.

2. For a description of industrial policies in the period 1917-1922, see Carr, *The Bolshevik Revolution 1917-1923*, Vol. 2 (Middlesex: Penguin, 1971), pp. 62-105 and 176-200; Lane, *Politics and Society in the USSR*, pp. 57-97; and Maurice Dobb, *Soviet Economic Development Since 1917* (London:

Routledge and Kegan Paul, 1966), p. 123. For a description of agricultural policies in this same period, see Carr, *Bolshevik Revolution,* Vol. 2, pp. 35–61 and 151–176.

3. Boris Meissner, "Social Change in Bolshevik Russia," in Meissner, *Social Change in the Soviet Union,* p. 27.

4. Quoted in James Bunyan and H. H. Fisher, *The Bolshevik Revolution 1917–1918: Documents and Materials* (Stanford, Cal.: Stanford University Press, 1934), p. 308.

5. Margaret Dewar, *Labor Policy in the USSR 1917–1918* (London: Royal Institute of International Affairs, 1956), p. 160.

6. Rimlinger, *Welfare Policy and Industrialization in Europe, America, and Russia,* p. 258.

7. Quoted in Chris Goodey, "Factory Committees and the Dictatorship of the Proletariat (1918)," *Critique. A Journal of Soviet Studies and Socialist Theory,* No. 3 (Autumn 1974):29.

8. Antonio Carlo, "The Socio-Economic Nature of the USSR," *Telos,* No. 21 (Fall 1974):2–86.

9. Quoted in Hyde, *Soviet Health Service,* p. 18.

10. Field, *Soviet Specialized Medicine,* p. 57.

11. For an account of the behavior of the Chilean Medical Association in response to policies that threatened its interests, see Vicente Navarro, "What Does Chile Mean: An Analysis of Events in the Health Sector Before, During, and After Allende's Administration," *Milbank Memorial Fund Quarterly* 52, 2 (1974):93–130.

12. Sigerist, *Medicine and Health in the Soviet Union,* p. 78.

13. For a detailed discussion of the composition and functions of the industrial workers' committees, see Goodey, "Factory Committees and the Dictatorship of the Proletariat."

14. For a current analysis of this position, see Stanley Aronowitz, "Left Wing Communism: The Reply to Lenin," in D. Howard and K. E. Klare (eds.), *The Unknown Dimension: European Marxism Since Lenin* (New York: Basic Books, 1972), p. 169.

15. Article 94 of the 1920 USSR *Constitution.*

16. Quoted in Carr, *Bolshevik Revolution,* Vol. 1, p. 154.

17. Quoted in Carr, *Bolshevik Revolution,* Vol. 2, p. 66.

18. See Maurice Brinton, "Factory Committees and the Dictatorship of the Proletariat," *Critique,* No. 4 (Spring 1975):78–86 for a discussion of such opposition.

19. Lenin, *Collected Works,* Vol. XVI, p. 120.

20. For an exposition of Lenin's views on the state, see his *State and Revolution*, in Lenin, *Collected Works*, Vol. XXV. And for a critique of Lenin's vision of political power and the state, see Antonio Carlo, "Lenin on the Party," *Telos*, No. 17 (1973):2-40, and Ralph Miliband, "The State and Revolution," in Paul Sweezy and Harry Magdoff (eds.), *Lenin Today* (New York: Monthly Review Press, 1970), pp. 77-90.

21. For a detailed account of Russian health conditions between 1918-1921, see Hyde, *Soviet Health Service*, pp. 47-67.

22. Quoted in N. A. Semaschko, *Health Protection in the USSR* (London, 1934), p. 39.

23. N. A. Semaschko, "The Soviet Revolution," *Deutsche Medizinische Wochenschrift* 50, 22 (1924):722-723. (In German)

24. Sigerist, *Medicine and Health in the Soviet Union*, p. 66.

25. For detailed information regarding changes in Soviet medical education during this period, see N. A. Semaschko, "The Soviet Health Services," *Deutsche Medizinische Wochenschrift* 50, 46 (1924):1587-1588. (In German)

26. Sigerist, *Medicine and Health in the Soviet Union*, p. 55.

27. National Academy of Sciences of the USSR, *Historical Bulletin* 23, 2 (1952). Also, visit by the author to the Archives of the History of Medicine, Semaschko Institute, 1974.

28. Quoted in Colletti, *From Rousseau to Lenin*, p. 221.

29. Ibid.

30. Lenin, *State and Revolution*, p. 357.

31. Ibid., p. 420.

Chapter 3
The New Economic Policy: 1921-1928

1. The best account of the state of the economy at the end of the period of War Communism is included in Dobb, *Soviet Economic Development Since 1917*, Chapters 5-6.

2. Lenin, *Selected Works*, Vol. III, p. 823.

3. For a detailed account of events during the NEP period, see Carr, *Bolshevik Revolution*, Vol. 2, pp. 280-357, and Carlo, "Socio-Economic Nature of the USSR." p. 53.

4. Meissner, "Social Change in Bolshevik Russia," p. 23.

5. Rimlinger, *Welfare Policy and Industrialization in Europe, America, and Russia*, p. 260.

6. Dewar, *Labor Policy in the USSR,* p. 160.

7. Semaschko, "Soviet Revolution," p. 722.

Chapter 4
The Period of Industrialization: 1928–1953

1. Trotsky had written, "For the final victory of socialism, for the organization of socialist production, the efforts of one country, especially a peasant country like ours, are not enough. For this we must have the efforts of the proletarians of several advanced countries." Leon Trotsky, *The Revolution Betrayed* (London: Pluto Press, 1957), p. 291.

2. Joseph Stalin, *Foundations of Leninism* (Moscow, 1934), p. 36.

3. Quoted in Meissner, "Social Change in Bolshevik Russia," p, 35.

4. Quoted in E. H. Carr, *Socialism in One Country,* Vol. 2 (Great Britain: Macmillan, 1958), p. 180.

5. Bettelheim, *Class Struggles in the USSR.*

6. Quoted in Ibid., p. 27. For a critique of Bettelheim, see Sweezy, "The Nature of Soviet Society," *Monthly Review* 26, 6 (1974): pp. 1-16; 26, 8 (1975):1-15. See also, Ralph Miliband, "Bettelheim and the USSR," *New Left Review,* No. 91 (1975):57.

7. Isaac Deutscher, *The Prophet Outcast. Trotsky: 1929-1940* (London; Oxford University Press, 1963), p. 66.

8. Gerschenkron, "Rate of Growth in Russia," pp. 161 and 166.

9. Stanovnik, *I Paesi in Via di Sviluppo nell' Economia Mondiale* (Milan, 1965), p. 49.

10. Lane, *Politics and Society in the USSR,* p. 66.

11. Meissner, "Social Change in Bolshevik Russia," p. 37.

12. Lane, *Politics and Society in the USSR,* p. 69.

13. Raymond Aron, *Eighteen Lectures on Industrial Society* (London: Weidenfeld and Nicolson, 1967).

14. J. Towster, *Political Power in the USSR, 1917-1947: The Theory and Structure of Government in the Soviet State* (London: Oxford University Press, 1948), p. 338.

15. Norton T. Dodge, *Women in the Soviet Economy* (Baltimore, Md.: The Johns Hopkins University Press, 1966).

16. Lane, *Politics and Society in the USSR,* p. 560.

17. Meissner, "Social Change in Bolshevik Russia," p. 38.

18. S. N. Prokopovich, *Russian Population Under the Soviets* (New York, 1952), p. 310.

19. Meissner, "Social Change in Bolshevik Russia," p. 36, and Dobb, *Soviet Economic Development Since 1917,* p. 312.

20. Lord Moran, *Churchill: The Struggle for Survival, 1940-1965* (Boston: Houghton Mifflin, 1966), p. 63.

21. Winston Churchill, *The Second World War: The Hinge of Fate* (Boston: Houghton Mifflin, 1950), p. 498.

22. R. W. Davies, "Planning for Rapid Growth in the USSR," *Economics of Planning* 5, 1-2 (1965):74-86.

23. Lane, *Politics and Society in the USSR,* p. 73.

24. A. Baykov, *The Development of the Soviet Economic System: An Essay on the Experience of Planning in the USSR* (London: Cambridge University Press, 1947), p. 326.

25. Roy Medvedev, *Let History Judge: The Origins and Consequences of Stalinism* (London: Macmillan, 1972), p. 239.

26. Ibid., p. 234.

27. Ralph Miliband, "Stalin and After," in Miliband and J. Saville (eds.), *The Socialist Register, 1973* (London: Merlin Press, 1974), p. 380.

28. Bettelheim, *Class Struggles in the USSR,* pp. 469-470.

29. Sweezy, "Nature of Soviet Society."

30. Meissner, "Social Change in Bolshevik Russia," p. 44.

31. Vicente Navarro, "The Industrialization of Fetishism or the Fetishism of Industrialization: A Critique of Ivan Illich," *Social Science and Medicine* 9, 7 (1975):351-363.

32. Navarro, "Social Policy Issues."

33. Cited in Meissner, "Social Change in Bolshevik Russia," p. 49. See also, Z. Katz, "Insights from Emigres and Soviet Sociological Studies on the Soviet Economy," in *Soviet Economic Prospects for the Seventies: A Compendium of Papers Submitted to the Joint Economic Committee of the 93rd Congress of the United States, June 23, 1973* (Washington, D.C.: Government Printing Office, 1973), pp. 87-120.

34. For a comprehensive review of changes in the social security scheme in this period, see Rimlinger, *Welfare Policy and Industrialization in Europe, America, and Russia,* p. 269 ff.; R. Abrahamson, "The Reoganization of Social Insurance Institutions in the USSR," *International Labour Review* 31, 3 (1935): 370; Maurice Dobb, *Social Insurance in the Soviet Union* (London: National Council for British-Soviet Unity, 1943); and J. Minkoff, "The Soviet Social Insurance System Since 1921," Ph.D. dissertation, Columbia University, 1959.

35. Quoted in Rimlinger, *Welfare Policy and Industrialization in Europe, America, and Russia,* p. 279.

36. Rimlinger, *Welfare Policy and Industrialization in Europe, America, and Russia,* p. 274.

37. S. M. Schwarz, *Labor in the Soviet Union* (New York: Praeger, 1951), p. 232.

38. Abrahamson, "Reorganization of Social Insurance Institutions in the USSR."

39. Cited in Hyde, *Soviet Health Service,* p. 98.

40. Ibid., p. 99.

41. Sigerist, *Medicine and Health in the Soviet Union,* p. 198.

42. For a full discussion of the situation of women in the Soviet Union, see Ibid., pp. 204-210, and Dodge, *Women in the Soviet Economy.*

43. G. Clark and N. Brinton, *Men, Medicine, and Food in the USSR* (London, 1936), p. 8.

44. T. M. Ryan, "Primary Medical Care in the Soviet Union," *International Journal of Health Services* 2, 2 (1972):243-253.

45. Hyde, *Soviet Health Service,* p. 127.

Chapter 5
Post-Stalinism: Khrushchev and After

1. Quoted in R. Schlesinger, "The New Pension Law," *Soviet Studies* 8, 3 (1957):307-314.

2. See, for example, the series by Martin Nicolaus, "Is the Soviet Union Capitalist?" *Guardian,* Nos. 1-17 (1975).

3. Carlo, "Socio-Economic Nature of the USSR," p. 75.

4. J. Levi, *Il Potere in Russia* (Bologna, 1967).

5. J. Colletti, "Il Metodo Liberman," *La Sinistra,* No. 1 (1967):18.

6. Carlo, "Socio-Economic Nature of the USSR," p. 17.

7. Meissner, "Social Change in Bolshevik Russia."

8. Carlo, "Socio-Economic Nature of the USSR," p. 75.

9. M. Sonin and E. Zhiltsov, "Economic Development and Employment in the Soviet Union," *International Labour Review* 96, 1 (1967):67-91.

10. Rimlinger, *Welfare Policy and Industrialization in Europe, America, and Russia,* p. 286.

11. Bernice Q. Madison, *Social Welfare in the Soviet Union* (Stanford, Cal.: Stanford University Press, 1968), p. 63.

12. Rimlinger, *Welfare Policy and Industrialization in Europe, America, and Russia.*

13. W. Salenson, "Social Security and Economic Development: A Quantitative Approach," *Industrial and Labour Relations Review* 21, 4 (1968):569.

14. Nicolaus, "Khrushchev Solidifies Hold" (Part 12 of "Is the Soviet Union Capitalist?") *Guardian* (May 7, 1975), p. 16.

15. Miliband, "Stalin and After," p. 383.

16. Paul Sweezy and Charles Bettelheim, *On the Transition to Socialism* (New York: Monthly Review Press, 1971).

Chapter 6
The Present Structure of the Soviet Health Sector

1. John Fry, *Medicine in Three Societies* (New York: American Elsevier, 1970), p. 27.

2. Ryan, "Primary Medical Care in the Soviet Union," p. 244.

3. Fry, *Medicine in Three Societies,* p. 27.

4. Ryan, "Primary Medical Care in the Soviet Union," p. 252.

5. Ibid.

6. Ibid.

7. Ibid.,

Chapter 7
The Health Labor Force in the Soviet Union

1. Meissner, "Social Change in Bolshevik Russia," p. 83.

2. T. B. Bottomore, *Classes in Modern Society* (London: Allen and Unwin, 1966), p. 47.

3. Meissner, "Social Change in Bolshevik Russia," p. 112.

4. This figure excludes collective farmers working in cooperatives. Mark Field, "Health Personnel in the Soviet Union: Achievements and Problems," *American Journal of Public Health* 56, 11 (1966):1904-1920.

5. Quoted in J. E. Muller et al., "The Soviet Health System," *New England Journal of Medicine* 286, 13 (1972):693-702.

6. D. Venediktov, "Union of Soviet Socialist Republics," in I. Douglas-Wilson and G. McLachlan (eds.), *Health Service Prospects* (Boston: Little Brown and Co., 1973).

7. John A. D. Cooper, "USSR and U.S. Health Policies," *New England Journal of Medicine* 286, 13 (1972):722-724.

8. J. Hogarth, *The Payment of the Physician: Some European Comparisons* (New York: Macmillan, 1963), p. 486.

9. Frederick Engels and Karl Marx, *Selected Correspondence* (Moscow: Foreign Languages Publishing House, 1956).

10. Quoted in Medvedev, *Let History Judge.*

11. Vicente Navarro, "Health Services in Cuba: An Initial Appraisal," *New England Journal of Medicine* 287, 19 (1972):954–959.

12. Quoted in Isaac Deutscher, *Stalin: A Political Biography* (New York: Vintage Books, 1960), p. 338.

13. Harold Lydall, *The Structure of Earnings* (Oxford: Clarendon Press, 1968), p. 142.

14. Medvedev, *Let History Judge,* p. 225.

15. M. D. Piradova, "The Role of Women in the Public Health Care System in the USSR," Paper presented at the International Conference on Women in Health, Department of Health, Education, and Welfare, Washington, D.C., June 1975, p. 10.

16. Vicente Navarro, "Women in Health Care," *New England Journal of Medicine* 292, 8 (1975):398–402.

17. Ibid.

18. *Yearbook for Labor Statistics* (Geneva: International Labour Organization, 1970–1975 editions).

19. P. H. Rossi and A. Inkeles, "Multidimensional Ratings of Occupations," *Sociometry* 20, 3 (1957):247.

Chapter 8
The Function of State Intervention in the Soviet Health Sector

1. Vicente Navarro, "The Political Economy of Medical Care," *International Journal of Health Services* 5, 1 (1975):65–94.

2. Milton Roemer, "Highlights of Soviet Health Services," *Milbank Memorial Fund Quarterly* 60 (1962):373–406.

3. Piradova, "Role of Women in the Public Health Care System in the USSR," p. 23.

Chapter 9
The Decision-Making, Planning, and Regulatory Machinery
in the Soviet Health System

1. "Rules of the CPSU" (Adopted at the 22nd Congress, 1961), *Soviet Booklet,* No. 82 (London, 1961).

2. Article 126, *Constitution of the USSR.*

3. Roy Medvedev, *On Socialist Democracy,* trans. E. DeKadt (New York: Alfred Knopf, 1975), p. 48.

4. The latter figures are based on the social background of members at the time they joined the Party. Lane, *Politics and Society in the USSR,* p. 135.

5. Boris Meissner, "Totalitarian Rule and Social Change," *Problems of Communism* 15, 6 (1966):59.

6. Lane, *Politics and Society in the USSR,* p. 140.

7. Venediktov, "Union of Soviet Socialist Republics," p. 231.

8. Ibid.

9. *National Health Planning in the USSR: Proceedings of an Interregional Travelling Seminar,* Sept. 16–Oct. 3, 1969, USSR (Geneva: World Health Organization, 1970), p. 15.

10. This information is based on discussions at the Semaschko Institute and on T. H. Rigby, *Communist Party Membership in the USSR, 1917–1967* (Princeton, N.J.: Princeton University Press, 1968), p. 43.

11. John Kenneth Galbraith, *The New Industrial State* (Boston: Houghton Mifflin Co., 1967), p. 389.

12. For an elaboration on this point, see Navarro, "Political Economy of Medical Care" and, by the same author, "Industrialization of Fetishism or the Fetishism of Industrialization."

Chapter 10
Epilogue: The Nature of the Soviet Union and Its Medicine

1. Carlo, "Lenin on the Party," p. 2.

2. Lenin, *What Is To Be Done?,* in *Collected Works,* Vol. V, p. 122.

3. Lenin, *Two Tactics,* in *Collected Works,* Vol. IX.

4. Colletti, *From Rousseau to Lenin,* p. 32.

5. Karl Marx, "Eighteenth of Brumaire," in *Selected Writings,* Vol. I (London: Lawrence and Wishart, 1962), p. 225.

6. Lenin, *Collected Works,* Vol. II, p. 32.

7. Bettelheim, *Class Struggles in the USSR.*

8. Che Guevara, "On the Budgetary Finance System," in Bertrand Silverman (ed.), *Man and Socialism in Cuba: The Great Debate* (New York: Atheneum, 1971).

9. Fidel Castro, "Speech of July 26, 1968," in M. Keuner and J. Petras (eds.), *Fidel Castro Speaks* (New York: Grove Press, 1969).

10. Navarro, "The Industrialization of Fetishism or the Fetishism of Industrialization."

11. Vicente Navarro, *Medicine Under Capitalism* (New York: Neale Watson Academic Publications, 1976).

12. Navarro, "What Does Chile Mean?"

13. Frederick Engels, *Anti-Dühring* (Moscow: Foreign Languages Publishing House, 1954).

14. Walter Kendall, *State Ownership, Workers' Control, and Socialism* (London: Square One Publications, 1972), p. 6.

15. D. Coates, *The Labour Party and the Struggle for Socialism* (London: Cambridge University Press, 1975).

16. P. Draper and T. Smart, "Social Science and Health Policy in the United Kingdom: Some Contributions of the Social Sciences to the Bureaucratization of the National Health Service," *International Journal of Health Services* 4, 3 (1974):453–470.

Bibliography

Abrahamson, R. "The Reorganization of Social Insurance Institutions in the USSR." *International Labour Review* 31, 3 (1935):370.

Annual Yearbook for Labour Statistics. Geneva: International Labour Organization, 1970–1975 editions.

Aron, R. *Eighteen Lectures on Industrial Society.* London: Weidenfeld and Nicolson, 1967.

Aronowitz, S. "Left Wing Communism: The Reply to Lenin." *The Unknown Dimension: European Marxism Since Lenin,* eds. D. Howard and K. E. Klare. New York: Basic Books, 1972.

Baykov, A. *The Development of the Soviet Economic System: An Essay on the Experience of Planning in the USSR.* London: Cambridge University Press, 1947.

Bettelheim, C. *Class Struggles in the USSR. First Period: 1917–1923.* New York: Monthly Review Press, 1976.

Birnbaum, N. *Toward a Critical Sociology.* New York: Oxford University Press, 1971.

Bottomore, T. B. *Classes in Modern Society.* London, 1966.

Braverman, H. "The Successes, the Failures, and the Prospects." *Fifty Years of Soviet Power.* New York: Monthly Review Press, 1967.

Brinton, M. "Factory Committees and the Dictatorship of the Proletariat." *Critique: A Journal of Soviet Studies and Socialist Theory* 4 (1975):78–86.

Bunyan, J. and Fisher, H. H. *The Bolshevik Revolution 1917–1918: Documents and Materials.* Stanford, Cal.: Stanford University Press, 1934.

Carlo, A. "Lenin on the Party." *Telos* 17 (1973):2–40.

_____. "The Socio-Economic Nature of the USSR." *Telos* 21 (1974):2–86.

Carr, E. H. *Socialism in One Country,* Vol. II. Great Britain: Macmillan, 1958.

_____. *The Bolshevik Revolution, 1917–1923,* Vols. I and II. Middlesex: Penguin Books, 1969 and 1971.

Castro, F. "Speech of July 26, 1968." *Fidel Castro Speaks,* eds. M. Keuner and J. Petras. New York: Grove Press, 1969.

Churchill, W. S. *The Second World War: The Hinge of Fate.* Boston, 1950.

Clark, G. and Brinton, N. *Men, Medicine, and Food in the USSR.* London, 1936.

Coates, D. *The Labour Party and the Struggle for Socialism.* London: Cambridge University Press, 1975.

Colletti, J. "Il Metodo Liberman," *La Sinistra* 1 (1967).

Colletti, L. *From Rousseau to Lenin: Studies in Ideology and Society.* New York: Monthly Review Press, 1972.

Cooper, J. A. D. "USSR and US Health Policies." *New England Journal of Medicine* 286, 13 (1972): 722-724.

Danilov, B. "Soviet Health Services." *Moscow News* (Economics, Science and Engineering Series), No. 16, 1967.

Davies, R. W. "Planning for Rapid Growth in the USSR." *Economics of Planning* 5 (1965):74-86.

Deutscher, I. *The Prophet Outcast. Trotsky: 1929-1940*. London: Oxford University Press, 1963.

_____. *Stalin: A Political Biography*. New York: Vintage Books, 1960.

Dewar, M. *Labor Policy in the USSR, 1917-1918*. London: Royal Institute of International Affairs, 1956.

Dobb, M. *Social Insurance in the Soviet Union*. London: National Council for British-Soviet Unity, 1943.

_____. *Soviet Economic Development Since 1917*. London: Routledge and Kegan Paul, 1966.

Dodge, N. T. *Women in the Soviet Economy*. Baltimore, Md.: Johns Hopkins University Press, 1966.

Draper, P. and Smart, T. "Social Science and Health Policy in the United Kingdom: Some Contributions of the Social Sciences to the Bureaucratization of the National Health Service." *International Journal of Health Services* 4, 3 (1974):453-470.

Eason, W. W. "Population Changes." *The Transformation of Russian Society*, ed. C. E. Black. Cambridge, Mass.: Harvard University Press, 1960.

Engels, F. *Anti-Dühring*. Moscow: Foreign Languages Publishing House, 1954.

Field, M. "American and Soviet Medical Manpower: Growth and Evolution." *International Journal of Health Services* 5, 3 (1975):455-474.

_____. "Health Personnel in the Soviet Union: Achievements and Problems." *American Journal of Public Health* 56, 11 (1966):1904-1920.

_____. *Soviet Specialized Medicine*. New York: The Free Press, 1967.

Frieden, N. M. "Physicians in Pre-Revolutionary Russia: Professionals or Servants of the State?" *Bulletin of the History of Medicine* 49, 1 (1975):20-29.

Fry, J. *Medicine in Three Societies*. New York: American Elsevier, 1970.

Galbraith, J. K. *The New Industrial State*. Boston: Houghton Mifflin, 1967.

Gerschenkron, A. "The Rate of Growth in Russia." *Journal of Economic History* 7, Suppl. (1947):146-155.

Goodey, C. "Factory Committees and the Dictatorship of the Proletariat." *Critique: A Journal of Soviet Studies and Socialist Theory* 3 (1974): 27-47.

Gorz, A. *Socialism and Revolution*. New York: Anchor Books, 1973.

_____. *Strategy for Labor: A Radical Proposal*. Boston: Beacon Press, 1964.

Guevara, C. "On the Budgetary Finance System." *Man and Socialism in Cuba: The Great Debate*, ed. B. Silverman. New York: Atheneum, 1971.

Hogarth, J. *The Payment of the Physician: Some European Comparisons*. New York: Macmillan, 1963.

Hosking, G. A. *The Russian Constitutional Experiment. Government and Duma 1907-1914*. London: Cambridge University Press, 1973.

Hyde, G. *The Soviet Health Service: A Historical and Comparative Study*. London: Lawrence and Wishart, 1974.

Katz, Z. "Insights from Emigrés and Soviet Sociological Studies on the Soviet Economy." *Soviet Economic Prospects for the Seventies: A Compendium of Papers Submitted to the Joint Economic Committee of the 93rd Congress of the United States*. Washington, D.C.: U.S. Government Printing Office, 1973.

Kendall, W. *State Ownership, Workers' Control and Socialism*. London: Square One Publications, 1972.

Lane, D. *Politics and Society in the USSR*. New York: Random House, 1970.

Lenin, V. I. *Collected Works*, Vols. II, V, IX, XVI, XVII, and XXV. Moscow: Foreign Languages Publishing House, 1963.

_____. *Selected Works*, Vol. III. New York: International Publishers, 1967.

Levi. J. *Il Potere in Russia*. Bologna, 1967.

Lyashchenko, P. I. *History of the National Economy of Russia*. New York: Macmillan, 1949.

Lydall, H. *The Structure of Earnings*. Oxford: Clarendon Press, 1968.

Madison, B. Q. *Social Welfare in the Soviet Union*. Stanford, Cal.: Stanford University Press, 1968.

_____. "The Organization of Welfare Services." *The Transformation of Russian Society*, ed. C. E. Black. Cambridge, Mass.: Harvard University Press, 1960.

Marx, K. *Selected Works,* Vol. 1. London: Lawrence and Wishart, 1962.

_____ and Engels, F. *Selected Correspondence*. Moscow, 1963.

McKeown, T. "A Historical Appraisal of the Medical Task." *Medical History and Medical Care*, eds. G. McLachlan and T. McKeown. London: Oxford University Press, 1971.

Medvedev, R. *Let History Judge: The Origins and Consequences of Stalinism*. London: Macmillan, 1972.

_____. *On Socialist Democracy*, trans. and ed. E. Dekadt. New York: Alfred Knopf, 1975.

Meissner, B. "Social Change in Bolshevik Russia." *Social Change in the Soviet Union*, ed. B. Meissner. Indiana: University of Notre Dame Press, 1972.

_____. "Totalitarian Rule and Social Change." *Problems of Communism* 15, 6 (1966):59.

Miliband, R. "The State and Revolution." *Lenin Today*, eds. P. M. Sweezy and H. Magdoff. New York: Monthly Review Press, 1970.

_____ . "Stalin and After." *The Socialist Register, 1973*, eds. R. Miliband and J. Saville. London: The Merlin Press, 1974.

_____ . "Bettelheim and the USSR." *New Left Review* 91 (1975):57-66.

Mills, C. W. *The Sociological Imagination*. New York: Grove Press, 1959.

Minkoff, J. *The Soviet Social Insurance System Since 1921*. Columbia University, Ph.D. dissertation, 1959.

Moran, L. *Churchill: The Struggle for Survival 1940-1965*. Boston: Houghton Mifflin, 1966.

Muller, J. E., et al. "The Soviet Health System." *New England Journal of Medicine* 286, 13 (1972):693-702.

Narodnoe Khoziaistvo v RSFSR, 1957: Statisticheski Sbornik. Moscow: Gosudarstvenoe Statisticheskoe Izdatelstvo, 1957.

Narodnoe Khoziaistvo v RSFSR, 1971: Statisticheskii Ezhegodnik. Moscow: Statistika, 1972.

Narodnoe Khoziaistvo v RSFSR, 1972: Statisticheskii Sbornik. Moscow: Statistika, 1972.

Narodnoe Khoziaistvo v SSR 1972: Statisticheskii Ezhegodnik. Moscow Statistika, 1973.

National Health Planning in the USSR: Proceedings of an Inter-Regional Travelling Seminar, USSR, September 16-October 3, 1969. Geneva: World Health Organization, 1970.

Navarro, V. "Health Services in Cuba: An Initial Appraisal." *New England Journal of Medicine* 287, 19 (1972):954-959.

_____ . "The Industrialization of Fetishism or the Fetishism of Industrialization: A Critique of Ivan Illich." *Social Science and Medicine* 9, 7 (1975):351-363.

_____ . *Medicine Under Capitalism*. New York: Neale Watson Academic Publications, 1976.

_____ . "The Political Economy of Medical Care." *International Journal of Health Services* 5, 1 (1975):65-94.

_____ . "Social Policy Issues: An Explanation of the Composition, Nature, and Functions of the Present Health Sector of the United States." *Bulletin of the New York Academy of Medicine* 51, 1 (1975):199-234.

_____ . "What Does Chile Mean: An Analysis of Events in the Health Sector Before, During, and After Allende's Administration." *Health and Society, Milbank Memorial Fund Quarterly* 52, 2 (1974):93-130.

_____ . "Women in Health Care." *New England Journal of Medicine* 290, 8 (1975):398-402.

Nicolaus, M. "Is the Soviet Union Capitalist?" *Guardian*, Nos. 1-17 (1975).

Piradova, M. D. "The Role of Women in the Public Health Care System in the USSR." Paper presented at the International Conference on Women in Health. U.S. Dept. of Health, Education and Welfare, Washington, D.C., June 1975.

Popov, G. A. "Outpatient and Hospital Care Facilities." *Public Health Papers*, No. 43. Geneva: World Health Organization, 1971.

_____. "The Problem of Posting and Utilizing Physicians." *Sovetskoe Zhravookhranenie*, No. 10 (1962).

Prokopovich, S. N. *Russian Population Under the Soviets*. New York, 1952.

Report of the United States Public Health Mission to the Union of Soviet Socialist Republics, August 13 to September 14, 1957. Washington, D.C.: U.S. Government Printing Office, 1959.

Results of the 1970 All-Union Census: Occupational Distribution of the Population of the USSR. Moscow: Central Statistical Administration, 1973.

Rigby, T. H. *Communist Party Membership in the USSR, 1917-1967*. Princeton, N. J.: Princeton University Press, 1968.

Rimlinger, G. V. *Welfare Policy and Industrialization in Europe, America, and Russia*. New York: John Wiley & Sons, 1971.

Roemer, M. "Highlights of Soviet Health Services." *Milbank Memorial Fund Quarterly* 40 (1962):373-406.

Ronaghy, H. A. and Solter, S. "Is the Chinese Barefoot Doctor Exportable to Rural Iran?" *Lancet* 1, 7870 (1974):1331-1333.

Rossi, P. H. and Inkeles, A. "Multidimensional Ratings of Occupations." *Sociometry* 20, 3 (1957):247.

Ruffmann, K. H. "Social Change in Russia Prior to the October Revolution." *Social Change in the Soviet Union*, ed. B. Meissner. Indiana: University of Notre Dame Press, 1972.

Ryan, T. M. "Primary Medical Care in the Soviet Union." *International Journal of Health Services* 2, 2 (1972):243-253.

Salenson, W. "Social Security and Economic Development: A Quantitative Approach," *Industrial and Labour Relations Review* 21, 4 (1968):569.

Schlesinger, R. "The New Pension Law." *Soviet Studies* 8, 3 (1957):307-314.

Schwarz, S. M. *Labor in the Soviet Union*. New York: Praeger, 1951.

Semaschko, N. A. "The Soviet Health Services," (in German). *Deutsche Medizinische Wochenschrift* 50, 46 (1924):1587-1588.

_____. "The Soviet Revolution," (in German). *Deutsche Medizinische Wochenschrift* 50, 22 (1924):722-723.

_____. *Health Protection in the USSR*. London, 1934.

Sigerist, H. *Medicine and Health in the Soviet Union*. New York: Citadel Press, 1947.

Sonin, M. and Zhiltsov, E. "Economic Development and Employment in the Soviet Union." *International Labour Review* 96, 1 (1967):67-91.

Stalin, J. *Foundations of Leninism*. Moscow, 1934.

Stanovnik, I. *Paesi in Via di Sviluppo Nell' Economia Mondiale*. Milan, 1965.

Sweezy, P. M. "The Nature of Soviet Society." *Monthly Review* 26, 6 (1974): 1-16.

———. "The Nature of Soviet Society." *Monthly Review* 26, 8 (1975):1-15.

——— and Bettelheim, C. *On the Transition to Socialism*. New York: Monthly Review Press, 1971.

Towster, J. *Political Power in the USSR, 1917-1947: The Theory and Structure of Government in the Soviet State*. New York: Oxford University Press, 1948.

Trotsky, L. *The Revolution Betrayed*. London: Plough Press, 1957.

Vadimov, T. *Socialist Principle of Payments According to Work*. Moscow, 1974.

Venediktov, D. "Union of Soviet Socialist Republics." *Health Service Prospects*, eds. I. Douglas-Wilson and G. McLachlan. Boston: Little, Brown and Company, 1973.

Von Laue, T. H. *Sergei Witte and the Industrialization of Russia*. New York: 1963.

Vucinich, A. "The State and the Local Community." *The Transformation of Russian Society*, ed. C. E. Black. Camoridge, Mass.: Harvard University Press, 1960.

Zdravookhranenie v SSSR, 1960: Statisticheskii Sbornik. Moscow: Gosstatizdat, 1960.

Index

Index

Abortion Act (1936), 45. *See also* Social security, women and

Abrahamson, R., 129, 130

Academy of Medical Sciences, 63, 93. *See also* Semaschko Institute

Agriculture: collectivization of, 36, 38–39, 42, 45–46, 67, 68t, 69t, 77; under Khrushchev, 53, 55–56; and NEP, 32–33; in pre-Soviet Russia, 3; subordination to industrialization, 36–37, 42, 109. *See also* Kolkhozs; Kulaks; Peasantry; Serfs

Alexander II, 1, 3, 9, 12. *See also* Zemstvo government

Aron, Raymond, 128

Bakunin, Mikhail, 36

Baykov, A., 129

Bettelheim, Charles, xvii, 40, 57, 109, 124, 128, 129, 131, 133

Bevan, Aneurin, 21

Birnbaum, Norman, xviii, 123

Bloody Sunday Massacre, 5

Bolshevik Party, 31, 40, 74, 106; economic blockade of, 16, 18, 24; economic policies of, 16n, 18; 1912 Prague meeting, 7, 16, 17; program of, 7–8, 15–16; socialist strategy of 6, 7, 24, 35; on social security and medicine, 8, 16, 17–29. *See also* Lenin; Revolution, Russian (of 1905); Revolution, Soviet (of 1917)

Bottomore, T. B., 67

Bourgeoisie, 4, 5, 7, 8, 14, 20, 23n, 31

Braverman, Harry, 123

Brinton, Maurice, 126

British Medical Association, 19, 21

Briton, N., 130

Bunyan, James, 126

Cabinet. *See* Council of Ministers

Cadets. *See* Constitutional Democratic Party

Carlo, Antonio, xvii, 54, 105, 126, 127, 130, 133

Carr, E. H., 16n, 124, 125, 126, 127, 128

Castro, Fidel, 110, 133

Central Council of Trade Unions (All-Russian), 20

Central Peoples' Commissariat of Health, 24–25

Central Planning Council, 62

Chekhov, Anton, 12

Chile, medicine in, under Allende, 20, 29, 115–116

Chilean Medical Association, 20

China, Peoples' Republic of, xv, xvi, 105; medicine in, xviii, 26, 29, 114, 115–116

Churchill, Winston, 39, 129

Clark, G., 130

Coates, D., 117, 134

Cold war, xv

Collectivization of land, 38; and productivity, 39; and rural health services, 45

Colletti, Lucio, xvi, xvii, 13, 107, 123, 125, 127, 130, 133

Commissariat of Health, 46

Commissariat of Labor, 33, 43

Communist Party of the Soviet Union (CPSU), 23, 55, 69, 74, 105; as branch of the state, 91–93; centralized political control in, 39–41, 109; composition of, 41, 57, 92–93, 103; Congresses of, 32, 33, 41, 42, 53; economic policies, 36–39, 45–46, 111–112; and health services, 42–51, 64, 98, 102–103, 111–113. *See also* Khrushchev; Lenin; Stalin, Stalinism; Trotsky

Community control: in the health sector, 29, 114, 116, 118. *See also* Chile; China; Cuba; Socialism; Workers' control

Constitutional Democratic Party (Cadets), 5, 6, 15, 16

143

About the Author

Vicente Navarro has taught health and social policy, political economy, and political sociology at academic institutions in Spain, Italy, France, Sweden, Great Britain, the United States, Canada, Cuba, Mexico, Argentina, and Colombia. He serves as advisor to a number of governments and international agencies. Among his recent books are *Medicine Under Capitalism* and the edited collection, *Health and Medical Care in the U.S.: A Critical Analysis.* He is also editor of the *International Journal of Health Services* and a founder of the International Group for Advanced Study of the Political Economy of Health. Dr. Navarro is presently professor of health and social policy at The Johns Hopkins University.